363.7
Br

K-1

Bruning, Nancy
Cities against nature

2660

DATE DUE			
OCT 13 '95			
OCT 27 '95			
NOV 17 '95			
MAR 22 '96			
MAY 27 '97			
MAR 2 1			
MAR 2 3			
cities against			
02-25-05			
MAR 2 8			

MEDIA CENTER
KENT MIDDLE SCHOOL
250 STADIUM WAY
KENTFIELD, CA 94904

DEMCO

Cities

Against Nature

CITIES AGAINST NATURE

Nancy Bruning

Educational Consultant
Helen J. Challand, Ph.D.
Professor of Science Education, National-Louis University

Technical Consultant
John Holtzclaw, Ph.D
Urban Sociologist
Chair, Sierra Club Transportation Subcommittee

CHILDRENS PRESS®
CHICAGO

A production of B&B Publishing, Inc.

Project Editor: Jean Blashfield Black
Designer: Elizabeth B. Graf
Cover Design: Margrit Fiddle
Artist: Valerie A. Valusek

Production Manager: Dave Conant
Photo Researcher: Marjorie Benson
Assistant Photo Researchers:
Kathy Brooks Parker
Terri Willis

Printed on Evergreen Gloss
50% recycled preconsumer waste
Binder's board made from 100% recycled material

Library of Congress Cataloging-in-Publication Data

Bruning, Nancy
    Cities against nature / Nancy Bruning
         p. cm. -- (Saving planet earth)
    Includes index.
    Summary: Examines the relationship of our cities to the environment and
suggests ways to build new cities on ecologically sound principles.
    ISBN 0-516-05510-0
    1. Urban ecology—Juvenile literature. 2. City planning—Environmental
aspects--Juvenile literature. [1. Urban ecology. 2. City planning. 3. Ecology.]
    I. Title. II. Series.
    HT241.B78 1992
    363.7'009173'2--dc20
                                     91-34604
                                        CIP
                                        AC

Cover photo—© Imtek Imagineering/Masterfile

TABLE OF CONTENTS

Chapter 1
Just Imagine

IMAGINE LIVING IN A CITY where people can walk or bike to almost anywhere they want to go: to school, to friends, to work, to the movies, and to shops. No one gets stuck in traffic, because there are so few cars. You can take buses, streetcars, ferries, and high-speed trains to places that are too far to reach by walking or riding your bicycle.

Imagine cleaner air, less noise, and lots of interesting things to do day and night. You know most of your neighbors, and people hang out and have fun in community gardens, parks, neighborhood markets, cafes, ice cream shops, and skating rinks. You can zip out of town and into the countryside on streets set aside just for biking and walking.

Imagine that there are no neighborhoods or streets where you feel scared or where you see a lot of sick people or sad people, or people who are so poor that they are homeless.

This imaginary city would be friendly, comfortable, and safe for you, your friends, and your family—and for the plants and animals that live in your area, too.

Sounds pretty good, doesn't it?

The Reality

Unfortunately, life in modern cities is usually nothing like this, although life in some cities once came pretty close. Our cities are changing rapidly, and in a disastrous direction—one that hurts both human lives and the environment.

Worldwide, most older city centers are becoming dirtier, and more congested and noisier from too much traffic, and sprinkled with decaying, neglected neighborhoods. But the major factors affecting cities and the environment are different in different parts of the world.

In the large cities of the industrial countries, such as New York, London, Toronto, and even Tokyo, the problem for the environment is that the cities are spreading out farther and farther. Such urban areas (*urban* comes from a Latin word meaning "city") generally consist of a city center, with buildings crowded together, residential areas, and surrounding towns called suburbs, where buildings are spread out over a lot more land and gradually merge into the countryside. For people to live so spread out, they must use cars and build roads.

Many cities in Asia, Latin America, and Africa have the same problem of decaying downtowns and spreading suburbs. But they have an additional problem, too—the shantytowns, or towns of shacks, that develop all along the fringes. Shantytowns are settlements where people who come to the city hoping for a better life often end up. When they can't find work or housing, they often build shacks out of whatever scrap material they can find. And there they stay, perhaps forever, as the "town" spreads around them.

Many children in Third World countries live in slums or shantytowns. These children in a Calcutta, India, slum do not have adequate food or housing. They struggle just to exist.

Western Cities. Big, smoggy cities of the developed nations, cities like Los Angeles, New York, Toronto, Tokyo, London, and Paris, can be lively and exciting places. The city center is a busy place of wonderful stores, office buildings where interesting work is done, museums, and entertainment.

But cities like these have too many people, too little public transportation, and too many cars. Such cities are difficult for their officials to take care of. Many of them

have serious problems with drugs, gangs, and other crime. There may be nice parks, but it may not be safe to walk in them after dark. Some neighborhoods are so deteriorated that they are abandoned by all but people who have nowhere else to go.

Such cities are caught in a circle of decay. Well-off people with money leave the city to live in the suburbs, taking their tax money with them. Because the city gets less money, there is little available to fix up the neighborhoods, so more people leave, and there is still less money. Finally, the only people left in the city are those with lots of money, who live right in the heart of the city, and low-income families who cannot afford to move away. It's very hard to break such a pattern.

But people in the suburbs still want to work in the city, or go shopping, or enjoy entertainment. Roads are built to carry suburban dwellers into the city more easily. When an expressway is cut through a neighborhood, air pollution from the passing cars rises, noise increases, and land values go down. Landlords and homeowners feel no need to fix things up, and so the neighborhood deteriorates even faster. On the roads themselves, the "rush hour" rushes nowhere.

Such cities expand into the suburbs, which appear to be

Big cities have many different faces. Many neighborhoods—decaying and ignored by officials (left)—are a bleak contrast to the bright lights of Times Square in New York City (right).

9

The suburbs of Los Angeles are always close to busy highways called freeways since most people depend on their cars to go practically everywhere.

clean and nice and peaceful. But many people find no excitement in suburban life. The places where things happen—the big city or maybe the shopping mall out on the highway—are reachable only by car.

In addition, people who study cities have found that although spread-out suburbs seem safe and relaxing, they are often more stressful than cities. They can be so quiet as to be boring because many residents feel isolated, and there's lots of tension in driving on crowded highways every day.

Cities in Developing Nations. It may not surprise you to learn that three-quarters of the people in developed nations like the United States and Canada now live in urban areas. But did you realize that more than half the people in less developed nations also live in cities—people in Africa, South America, and Asia?

Most cities in these less developed, or Third World, nations have existed for a long time, but, unlike industrialized cities, they only recently started to grow. And then they grew so rapidly that there has been no time or resources to make the growth smooth or healthy. To people in the country who suffer great poverty, there appears to be hope for a better life in the cities, even in the shantytowns.

Since 1970, many cities have expanded greatly. Mexico

City had 9 million in 1970 and is expected to reach at least 27 million by the year 2000. São Paulo, Brazil, is almost as bad. It had 8 million people in 1970 and is expected to reach 24 million. Jakarta, Indonesia, will go from 4 million to 13 million. Much of the growth is in shantytowns, although no one really knows how many people live in them. One of Mexico City's shantytowns is actually Mexico's fourth largest city.

In most Latin American and African countries, cities are growing at a rate of 10 percent each year. That is so fast that there is no time or money to build the city facilities that residents need. And still people keep moving in from the countryside.

Worldwide, the people in shantytowns live without jobs, without water, without sanitary facilities, without schools, without transportation, without medical care.

But they are not without hope. Even without real jobs, families—starting from the youngest child—can usually get some money by scrounging items from the trash dumps, running errands for people, begging, or from prostitution. They get more money than they would if they had stayed in the countryside. That probably will not last, however,

Shanties can be built anywhere that space and materials are available. These shanties, located on the roof of an old building, house two migrant families in Mexico City.

11

Many families from rural El Salvador have moved to San Salvador to escape poverty. But they only end up in the greater poverty of "squatter" settlements.

because there are too many people willing to work for too little money. Urban poverty will soon be a greater problem than rural poverty.

But people keep hoping, and the cities keep growing. The World Health Organization predicts that by the year 2000, 77 percent of all families in African cities will live in poverty. UNICEF, the United Nations children's fund, has warned that millions of today's children are growing up in conditions that will not allow them to grow either physically or mentally. Many of them won't even live to grow up at all because life in the shantytowns brings killing diseases.

Argentinian professor Jorge E. Hardoy wrote, "We are blindly passing to the future generations urban environments which are rapidly deteriorating and cities so populous that the option for future generations will be limited."

Cities and the Environment

People are starting to realize that cities often create an unhealthy environment for the people who live in them. But now city-related problems are reaching beyond the cities themselves. Today's cities are, in fact, unhealthy for the environment of the whole planet.

The way we are living is destroying resources—our water, air, and energy sources—as well as people and other living things. Every minute, our cars add tons of pollutants to the air we breathe.

Today, we are thinking about our cities and our environment in a new way. Our environment is affected not only by the way we treat trees and birds and oceans, but also by the way people treat each other. Here, too, today's cities contribute to our problems.

We hardly know our own neighbors. We're taught to be afraid of strangers and of people who seem different from us. We are warned to stay out of certain neighborhoods because drugs are there, muggers are there, and people often get robbed or hurt . . . or both.

We have learned how important it is to work for a cleaner, safer world. We know we must change some of our personal habits. We know we should recycle more, use less water, and rely less on cars. We know we should learn to understand nature and accept that we are part of it. We don't want to feel afraid of other people. But the way cities are built makes it difficult to improve our habits and our ways of thinking.

The cities of the Third World are unhealthy for individuals, but they are not as unhealthy for the Earth's environment as cities in North America are. Cities in the industrialized world are inhabited by people who overuse the planet's resources, pollute the atmosphere, discard huge quantities of waste, and then ask for more. These are the places that must change so that they work *with* the natural world instead of *against* it. We need to understand that what happens to one place will eventually affect us all.

Naturalist John Muir said a hundred years ago: "When one tugs at a single thing in nature, he finds it attached to the rest of the world."

Crime, poverty, and violence are a way of life in parts of Washington, D.C. This business was looted and burned during a riot. The rubble still stands.

Chapter 2

How Our
Cities Grew . . .
and Grew . . .
and Grew

WE CAN BETTER UNDERSTAND how today's cities came to be so unhealthy and such a danger to the natural environment if we go back in history. Let's take a look at how the very first cities came to be.

From the beginning, cities were linked with the way people lived. The way people behaved and the things they believed in shaped their towns and cities. In turn, people themselves were shaped by their communities.

Familyville—The Hunter-Gatherers

About 2 or $2^1/_2$ million years ago, human beings lived in very small groups. These societies were based on the family or tribe. They included members of the immediate and extended family—parents, children, grandparents, great-grandparents, aunts, uncles, cousins, and other even more distant relatives.

These early humans were hunter-gatherers, people who depended on wild plants and animals to supply their needs. They were nomadic. They wandered from place to place, following the changing supply of food, water, and good weather. They lived close to nature and were a part of it.

People who lived in these ancient societies gathered fruits, nuts, vegetables, and berries. They hunted wild animals, which they brought back to the camp to share. They had to plan together and work together to hunt and gather and prepare the food.

The early nomads had few possessions other than some hunting weapons, clothes, and containers. They were always on the move, and too many possessions were a burden.

Anthropologists (scientists who study the development

American Indians gathered the food they needed each year without destroying the land or the wildlife. These Indians are collecting wild rice.

and customs of people) think these early people got most of their happiness and satisfaction from close family relationships. They also enjoyed visiting with friends, dancing and storytelling, teaching and learning. They created and followed religious rituals, and they made useful and beautiful tools and jewelry.

Hunter-gatherer groups were small—perhaps not more than 40 people. We used to think their lives must have been hard, but new evidence shows that this was probably not so. They may have spent as little as 12 to 19 hours a week actually gathering and hunting. The rest of the time was spent socializing, playing, and resting.

Many anthropologists believe that this era was the only time that humans existed in balance with their environment. They took only what they needed to survive—enough food and water, and perhaps animal skins to make clothing and plants to make temporary shelters.

Humans Settle Down

As humans evolved and their power to think, learn, and invent new things increased, they were able to adapt to many different environments. Eventually, they were able to change their environment to suit themselves.

An important change in history and our relationship to the environment occurred when humans began to plant and cultivate crops.

Instead of going into the forest to gather food, they planted seeds in a specific place and then harvested the crop.

They not only controlled plant life, they also began to control animals by domesticating them—feeding them and training them to help with certain tasks.

With a more reliable food supply, the number of people in a group could safely grow. More babies were born because they didn't have to be carried everywhere. And more babies lived to grow up because staying in one place was safer. Human settlements became bigger and more complex, and so did the societies within them.

Rather than everyone participating in the hunting, gathering, and preparation of food, people began to specialize in doing different things. They traded things they grew or made for things that other people grew or made, or for the services they performed. Small settlements became villages, and villages began to expand into towns and cities.

About 3,000 to 5,000 years ago, the first real cities began to appear. They flourished in Egypt, India, China, and Mesopotamia (the area between the Tigris and Euphrates rivers, now in Iraq). Cities became vital, diverse places to live, with politics, commerce, culture, religious rituals, crafts, and busy markets and city centers.

The Zulus had many self-sufficient settlements in southern Africa. Pottery was made to use in the village or to trade with other settlements.

17

The "Golden Age" of Cities

The first settlements, villages, towns, and cities grew where resources were most plentiful. They were near good soil, near water, and near places where domesticated animals could thrive and provide food, clothing, and labor.

Although people walked everywhere, the best cities were located in places with good transportation. By settling along rivers, around bays, and near mountain passes, people could travel to other areas and exchange goods, services, and information. People got news by word of mouth—one person telling another.

Most people worked in the city or the neighborhood they lived in—and often they worked right in their own homes. Craftspeople such as potters, weavers, and leather workers made items they used themselves or traded for other goods. People knew their neighbors, and family members lived close to each other. Farmland surrounded the cities, and most things people needed were grown nearby or made in the city.

Cities tended to be compact in design because transportation, water, and food were limited. Even when new areas (suburbs) developed outside the city, they were within walking distance. The city center had a large marketplace, where people sold what they made or grew, and visited with other people. There was usually lively entertainment, too—music, dancing, and theater.

Generally, these city dwellers wasted little. Human and animal power were the main sources of energy, and human and animal waste, and cooking and heating fires were probably the only sources of pollution. People had their own gardens, as well as access to the country and nearby suburbs

with orchards, vineyards, fish-filled streams, and open fields and forests. The narrow streets of the city were balanced with open spaces.

Not Everything Was Wonderful. Some people refer to this time as the "Golden Age of Cities." But we can't ignore the fact that many of these cities had problems.

For example, although people in general used few natural resources, this was not always the case. The residents of the Pueblo Indian village of Mesa Verde in southern Colorado stripped the trees for miles around to use as firewood. Ancient Rome was very crowded. The Romans built and rebuilt buildings up to ten stories high, mainly of wood, at the cost of nearby forests. Mesopotamian cities such as Baghdad also destroyed the forests to build urban structures. The forest loss caused the soil to erode and the Tigris-Euphrates Valley to silt up.

Houses in these early and medieval cities were small. Heating was a problem in winter so the whole family usually slept together. There was little privacy and no bathrooms. Human and animal waste was often dumped into the streets. In fact, this practice continued until the last century. However, the waste was organic and could be used to fertilize soil in gardens and fields.

Machines Change Everything: The Industrial Revolution

During the late 1700s, however, many cities began to change drastically because of the invention of the steam-powered engine. This mechanical device, which was fueled by burning coal, made factories possible. The craftsman who made things one at a time, by hand, became a creature of the past. Factories enabled people to make thousands of things by machine.

Country people streamed into cities to get jobs in the new factories. They were part of what came to be called the Industrial Revolution.

Starting in the 1840s, steam engines also began to power railroads, which were built between cities. New cities grew up along railroad lines. Faster travel was now possible between cities, and people didn't need rivers and oceans for transportation. Cities could be built anywhere!

At the same time, agriculture was also changing. People who spent their days in factories needed someone else to grow food for them. Also, as the population increased, so did the demand for food.

Farms began to operate more like factories. The farmers needed other people to help them, but machines such as steam-powered tractors began to do more of the work. And more country people headed for the cities.

These drastic changes first occurred in Great Britain, then Western Europe, and finally the United States. Other parts of the world followed. Japan, for example, went through its industrial revolution in the early 1900s.

The Third World countries of Africa, Latin America, and Asia are just now industrializing, which is why they are called developing countries. Many people are hoping that the developing nations will be able to avoid some of the environmental problems that were created by the Western nations as they industrialized.

Industrialization transformed people's lives. Cities became unpleasant places to live in, and they had a larger impact on the environment. New factory towns, for example, were often built near waterfronts. The waterways provided lots of water for the factories. But rivers and lakes were also convenient places to dump wastes.

Sewage, garbage, and dirty air became problems. Men, women—and even children—were forced to work long hours in dark, unsafe factories. They breathed the city air, which had become black with soot from the coal the factories burned to run the machines. Polluted air does not stay nicely put above the factories and highways where it originates. It is caught up by the winds that circle the planet and transported throughout the atmosphere.

Technology allowed us to increase our population and

Brazil's current "industrial revolution" is causing serious environmental problems—problems that Japan, Europe, and North America faced in the early 1900s.

have a huge impact on our environment. As one scientist put it, "People have ruined parts of the planet before. But now we realize we can harm the *entire* planet."

City people's lives gradually focused more and more on work. Fewer people worked at home, so old people were not taken care of. Buildings were not repaired, and many neighborhoods became run down. In spite of working long hours, wages were low. People could not afford to buy new houses, so families lived in overcrowded conditions. Sickness was widespread due to overwork, poor nutrition, poor sanitation, and pollution. Once a contagious disease started, it could spread through the crowded cities like wildfire.

Life became a different kind of struggle. The poverty of the cities became as bad as the poverty that drove people to the cities in the first place.

Early Suburbs—Escape to the Edge

In the United States, wealthy city people began to build houses in the countryside for summer vacations and weekend visits. They were able to escape from the city, and felt pulled toward the idea of unspoiled nature, cleaner air, better health, quiet surroundings, and wide-open space.

Many people moved out of the city and became commuters—they traveled back and forth to work. They found the journey worth the effort, because they could live and raise their children in more pleasant surroundings.

At first, they commuted by horse and carriage. But the invention of the steam-engine train and the electric street car brought a full-blown migration to the suburbs.

As more people moved to the suburbs, the cities began to build rail lines for streetcars, called trolleys. The first were

horse drawn, followed by cable cars like those still operating in San Francisco, and later powered from overhead electric lines. Later, motor buses and electric trolley buses powered from overhead lines were also used.

The first ring of new homes around the outside of the city became known as the "trolley suburb." Houses and stores in the trolley suburb were clustered within walking distance of trolley and commuter railway lines.

As public transportation became cheaper, more people were able to afford it. Walking distance no longer limited how far a person could travel, or how big a city could grow. Americans took about 24 billion trips a year on trolleys and buses during World War II, from 1941 to 1945. But that changed quickly.

Cars Drive into Our Lives

In the early twentieth century, automobiles were novelties, luxuries that only the rich could afford. Cars had little impact on the environment or on our lives. They didn't use

Electric streetcars carried large numbers of people from outlying areas into Toronto, Canada, for work and shopping. Streetcars could be loaded easily and gave off no smelly fumes.

up much steel or other materials, they didn't need many roads, and they didn't burn up much gas.

But then Henry Ford developed mass production, starting about 1915. Cars put together on assembly lines became cheaper. Soon, there were so many cars that they replaced trains and electric trolleys. Now the average American could afford a car. This fact gradually transformed cities into noisy, polluted, congested places. The trolley suburbs became the far-flung sprawling suburbs of today, suburbs that depend entirely on people using cars.

A lot of things happened about the same time to make life in suburbia possible.

Starting in the 1930s, the auto, oil, steel, and tire industries bought up more than a hundred electric trolley systems and took them apart. After tearing the trolley tracks out of the ground and removing the overhead electric lines, they replaced the trolleys with gasoline-burning buses.

But people didn't like the buses as much as they liked the trolleys, so the buses weren't used as much. Without satisfactory public transportation, people began to demand private cars. Cars were becoming the only way that people could get to work.

With the completion of the Don Valley Parkway after World War II, the car-dependent suburbs of Toronto, Canada, grew quickly.

Everyone wanted a car. They were fast. They went door to door. They represented the freedom to go anywhere there was a road. And soon there were roads everywhere. In the United States, building cars, roads, and new suburban houses created jobs for 11 million returning World War II veterans. The govern-

ment played its part by using tax money to build the freeways, including a huge project called the Interstate Highway System—40,000 miles (64,000 kilometers) of highways.

Gasoline to power the cars was cheap—only 12 cents a gallon (3.8 liters) in the 1930s. The air was still clean. And roads had not begun to consume the land.

No one realized what a problem cars would become.

Suburbs such as this part of Toronto, Canada, offered industrial workers the "good" life. But they also created boring, uniform areas with houses exactly alike and few open spaces.

The Spread of Sprawl

This suburban explosion seemed like a good idea at the time. But the expanding suburbs meant we needed more cars and more freeways, which led to still more suburbs, and so on. Each fed off the other, creating the type of expanded, sprawling city that is developing all over the world today.

As the suburbs flourished, the city centers began to decay. Middle-class people, mostly white, moved out of the cities and took their money with them. But they still commuted into the business districts of the cities to work.

Poor people and minorities, mostly African Americans and immigrants, were left behind in decaying "bad" neighborhoods. But the business areas continued to boom.

The American Dream. At first, the suburbs looked like the best of both worlds—living in the city and the country at the same time. Every family had its own house and car. Every house had its own garage—frequently big enough to hold two or three cars—its own radio and TV, its own green lawn, and its own washer and dryer. Young couples enjoyed living in a nice, new house, in a clean, quiet neighborhood with other young couples just like themselves.

FACT

In 1800, about 6 percent of the American population lived in cities. One hundred years later, the figure had risen to 40 percent. In 1990, about 80 percent of the 250 million people in the United States lived in cities and their suburbs.

Suburban life seemed so ideal that it became a way of life that people called "The American Dream." But gradually, so many people commuted by car to the city that highways became congested, or crowded.

One solution to this problem would have been to invest money in the city. If cities had built more affordable houses, better schools, and safe, pleasant places to meet and play in; if they had invested in local businesses and provided good jobs; and if they had kept the streets and water and sewage systems in good repair, they would have been more appealing places to live. Needless to say, this didn't happen in many places.

The Dream Becomes a Nightmare for the City

Instead, many businesses decided that moving to the suburbs was the answer, so they, too, began to leave the cities. Land was cheaper in the suburbs, and it was far from urban decay. And, of course, many people thought that such moves would reduce the traffic problems.

So banks took money that inner-city people had saved and invested it in suburbs, where it seemed safer. Along with the government, they poured money into suburban single-family homes, into roads and police, into water and sewage systems.

Auto companies spend $5 billion annually in the United States for advertising alone, while the whole national transit budget is only $3.2 billion.

City centers got even worse. Buildings got rundown, schools were overcrowded or closed, businesses shut, and there were fewer police officers, fire fighters, transit lines, and other services needed to keep the city safe and running.

"Sorry, No Money." Instead of putting money into city centers and helping people with low incomes buy and repair old homes, the U.S. government and industry encouraged the building of new houses. They thought that "new" was better because new construction meant jobs and money for new materials. It meant buying land, and creating more money and jobs to build roads and manufacture new cars.

So the government made it easy for banks to give low-interest mortgages for suburban homes and difficult for

The U.S. federal government encourages new home construction because it means more jobs and more money in the economy. Inner-city housing is often left to deteriorate while more prosperous residents move to the suburbs.

27

banks to lend money for city homes. This policy was called "red-lining" because the bankers drew red lines on their maps around undesirable neighborhoods.

Cars in the Suburbs

Eventually, so many businesses moved to the suburbs that people "cross-commuted." Instead of driving from a suburban home to work in the city, they drove from one suburb to another. Now these roads, far from the city center, are congested, too.

Early in the history of the car, a manufacturer predicted that there would never be more than 1 million cars in the world. Only fifteen years later, there were more than that. In 1990 there were almost 500 million cars worldwide—with one-third of these owned by Americans. The experts predict that in thirty more years, traffic will double to almost a *billion* cars.

Fifty years after the car-dependent suburb was invented, more than 25 million Americans commute each day between homes and jobs, both in the suburbs. Such commuting alone accounts for a great deal of our daily car trips. And people

In the United States, most gasoline tax money goes for building roads. Less than one-tenth is spent on creating better mass transit. Other tax money goes to maintain roads and bridges and to provide police, ambulance, and fire protection to commuters.

usually travel alone in their cars. Only 5 percent of Americans use public transportation to get to work.

In many cities, parts of the lively, exciting city center are beginning to turn into deadly, scary places. Where do most people go to shop, play, see each other, and take in a movie? To the suburban mall, not to the city. And how do most people get where they want to go? By car.

Changing Patterns

The suburb was invented for the "typical American family." But now there is no typical family, no typical way of life. Most mothers work outside the home. Many families have a single parent who has to work as well as see that the children are taken care of.

Many families have no children. There are many older people who can't drive cars, and many poor people who can't afford them. And there are many people who live alone and need small homes close to other people.

Because of these changing patterns, the suburban way of building, and the suburban way of life, don't make sense anymore. Suburbs are no longer practical, or needed—or even wanted—by most people. They waste our resources, pollute our planet, hurt our health, and hurt nature.

World Cities

As you'll see in the next chapters, much of the physical and human environmental problems in developed, industrialized countries are related to our sprawling cities and our dependence on cars. A lot of these problems are local or regional, but because everything on Earth is connected, such cities are also having a global impact.

MEGACITIES OF THE YEAR 2000	1985 Population (in millions)	Estimated Population by 2000	Metropolitan Area (in square miles)	Density (people per square mile) 1985	Density (people per square mile) 2000
Mexico City, Mexico	17.3	25.8	883	19,592	29,219
São Paulo, Brazil	15.9	24.0	3,101	5,127	7,739
Tokyo, Japan	18.8	20.2	834	22,542	24,220
Calcutta, India	11.0	16.5	533	20,638	30,957
Greater Bombay, India	10.1	16.0	233	43,348	68,670
New York, New York	15.6	15.8	1,384	11,272	11,416
Seoul, South Korea	10.3	13.8	234	44,017	58,974
Teheran, Iran	7.5	13.6	N/A		
Rio de Janeiro, Brazil	10.4	13.3	2,496	4,167	5,328
Shanghai, China	11.8	13.3	2,383	4,951	5,581
Buenos Aires, Argentina	10.9	13.2	1,497	7,281	8,817
Delhi, India	7.4	12.0	572	12,937	23,076
Jakarta, Indonesia	7.9	11.2	*254		
Karachi, Pakistan	6.7	11.1	560	11,964	21,428
Dacca, Bangladesh	4.9	11.1	N/A		
Manila, The Philippines	7.0	11.0	246	28,455	45,121
Cairo, Egypt	7.7	10.7	*83		
Los Angeles, California	10.0	10.5	4,070	2,457	2,702
Bangkok, Thailand	6.1	10.5	604	10,099	17,715
London, England	10.4	10.4	610	17,049	17,213
Osaka, Japan	9.4	10.4	721	13,037	14,563
Beijing, China	9.1	9.1	6,490	1,402	1,602
Moscow, Russia	9.0	9.1	386	23,316	26,942

*city area only   N/A – not available

In 1800, less than 2 percent of the world's population lived in large cities. In 1950, 13 percent did. In the year 2000, more than 50 percent of the world's people will inhabit cities. At least 23 of those cities will be "megacities," with over 10 million people each, and most of those will be in developing countries.

Today, the trouble isn't limited just to the big, rich, developed countries like the United States and Canada. The developing countries are seeing urban-related environmental problems. Cities in Third World countries are growing by leaps and bounds, but without much planning. It has been said that it is poverty, not planning, that is determining the shape of Third World cities.

Millions of country people, frustrated by land that won't produce, are leaving the rural areas and heading for the cities. Few of them have any skills that will get them jobs. Instead, they live in poverty on the fringes of the cities. In these Third World countries, urban sprawl does not come from trim, green suburbs, but from shantytowns that, week by week, year by year, become permanent towns that are incorporated into the city.

In Third World cities, where public transportation may exist but often does not function properly, traffic is becoming a major problem. Motor vehicles can be caught in traffic jams for hours, engines running, spewing black pollutants into the air. The traffic doesn't consist, however, of just cars and trucks and buses. It also includes horses, cattle, rickshaws, and millions of bicycles. The response, unfortunately, is to build more roads.

Experts believe that the number of cars in Europe will double by the year 2010. Manufacturers are hoping that Eastern Europe and the former Soviet Union will follow. India and China currently have 38 percent of the world's population, but less than 0.5 percent of its cars. By 2010, the number of cars in Asia and Latin America will probably double and redouble.

FACT

The industrialized world uses over 50 percent of the world's energy resources. Experts predict that if the whole world spent as much energy as North Americans do, natural energy sources would be all used up by the year 2004.

Our car-centered, energy-gobbling way of life can't go on forever. The problems it is causing today in our environment and among our people will get worse, especially as cities in developing nations follow our lead. Instead of making the world a better place to live, cars and cities are destroying the environment and millions of people.

Chapter 3

Today's Cities Waste Our Resources

A RESOURCE IS ANYTHING that we can use to support us or help us in some way. In a sense, resources are like having money in the bank.

Our planet has an abundance of natural resources that keep us alive and healthy. Until the Industrial Revolution, human beings used very little of these resources—we "lived lightly" on the Earth.

But now, not only are there many more of us, but each of us is using, on average, much more of Earth's resources. In fact, many of us are using much more than we need—we are wasting our fuel, our land, our water, and our people. We take more out of our "bank account" than we put in—and one day our account could be empty.

The way we design and build our cities and suburbs has forced us to be dependent on cars, highways, and oil.

Using all major world cities to come up with an average, a city of 9 million inhabitants has been found to use up 5.6 million metric tons of water, 18,000 metric tons of food, and 85,500 metric tons of fuel every day. It produces 4.5 million metric tons of wastewater, 18,000 metric tons of solid wastes, and 8,550 metric tons of air pollutants every day.

FACT

We use concrete, coal, iron, slag, clay pipe, and explosives to build and maintain highways. We use tons of steel, aluminum, rubber, and plastic to make cars. A General Motors official once said, "As a consumer of raw materials, the automobile has no equal in the history of mankind."

It takes energy to get work done, to move things around,

When fossil fuels burn they are gone forever, unlike renewable (and nonpolluting) energy sources such as the sun, wind, and water.

and to make things. We have many forms of energy, including people power (from the food we eat) and solar power (from the sun). But our main source of energy today is burning fossil fuels.

Fossil fuels are coal, oil, and natural gas. They were created from fossils—the remains of living things—by natural processes over millions of years. Century after century in prehistoric times, plants died and fell into the swamps of ancient Earth. The partially decayed plants were compressed and gradually changed into the fuels we dig out of the Earth today.

We use oil to run cars, to heat buildings, to turn into chemicals, especially plastics and medicines. Considering all the things we use petroleum for, it's hard to imagine a world without it. The oil left in the Earth won't last much longer. Yet, we continue to burn it as if tomorrow will never come.

Fuel for Cars

The United States, with only 5 percent of the world's population, uses 25 percent of the world's fuel. Much of it is burned in the engines of our cars and trucks. Japan uses only one-eleventh of the amount of gasoline that the United States does. Automobiles burn 70 percent of the fossil fuel used in cities—and 45 percent of all the oil taken from the Earth.

FACT

Americans are so dependent on their cars and trucks that in one year, 1990, they drove *2 trillion miles*—that's 2,000,000,000,000 miles, or 3,218,600,000,000 kilometers—364 times the distance to the planet Pluto and back again.

In Los Angeles, where urban sprawl is a way of life, traffic is so congested that drivers now use 1 of every 4 gallons (3.7 of every 15.14 liters) of gasoline just idling their cars in traffic jams. How ironic that Los Angeles once had what some people think was the best mass-transit system in the country. But Los Angeles was one of the cities where the electric trolley systems were dismantled.

Los Angeles' crowded freeways often look like huge, slow-moving parking lots. Some commuters spend 4 to 5 hours each day driving to and from work.

The situation in Los Angeles might get even worse—it has been estimated that the average driving speed in Los Angeles will be down to 15 miles (24 kilometers) per hour by the year 2000. However, in 1988, a local law was passed requiring all companies with more than 100 employees to develop plans for carpooling by their staff. That will help.

By 2005, traffic delays on America's highways are expected to be four times as bad as they are now!

Fuel for Transporting Goods from Far Away

The availability of transportation is what makes cities possible, and yet that transportation uses up the fuel supplies of the world. Almost all the things we eat, drink, wear, or play with come from far away. In the United States and Canada, the shoes people wear may have been made in Italy or Taiwan or South America; their TV sets in Japan or Korea; and their furniture on the other side of the country.

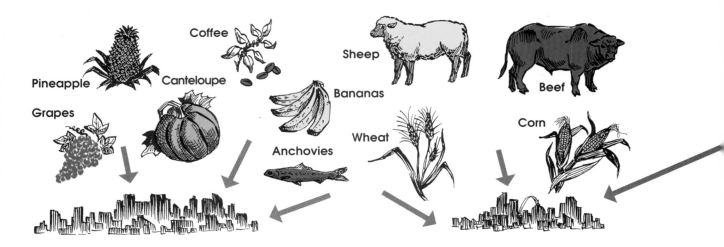

An Earth Experience

Meals on Wheels

Make a list of every kind and brand of food you eat in one day. If you have eaten a balanced diet, this will include meat, dairy products, fruit, vegetables, and breads or cereals. Don't forget to include salt, pepper, spices, salad dressing, juice, pop, sugar, and other snacks.

Using your list, read the labels on the cans, cartons, or jars on your pantry shelf. Where was each food processed for shipment? Go to the grocery store where your family shops to get the information. Ask the produce manager where the fresh fruits and vegetables were grown. Chances are the pineapple is from Hawaii, the

Food travels so far because so few of us now grow or raise our own food, and suburban developments are built over good farmland. Shipping distances grew from tens of miles to thousands. On the average, the various items Americans eat every day—from flour to juice to vegetables— have traveled 1,500 miles (2,414 kilometers) by the time they reach our plates! This practice is one that wastes the most natural resources.

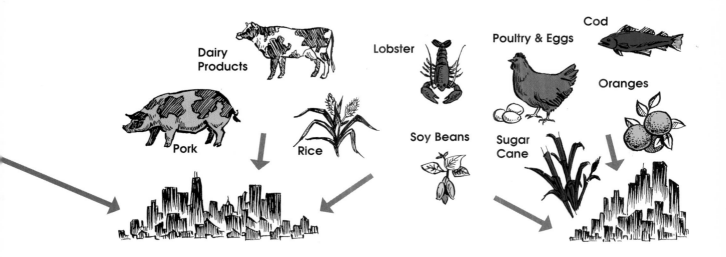

oranges from Florida, and the potatoes from Idaho.

Now locate each place on a map. Figure out how many miles each food traveled to get to you. Can you also figure out the method of transportation needed for each food? For example, the salmon in the Pacific Ocean comes in to the coast by boat. It is then transported by truck or rail to the nearest canning plant. How did it get from there to your state? Finally, did you drive or walk to the supermarket to buy the salmon?

Add up the mileage your food has traveled for just one day's meals. How can this use of fossil fuels be reduced? What can you do about reducing it?

Our government and economic system encouraged farms to become bigger and bigger. Today, most of our food is raised on huge, factory-like farms run by "agri-business" corporations instead of farmers. They use vast amounts of petroleum-based chemicals, artificial fertilizers, pesticides, water for irrigation, and even powerful drugs that speed up the growth of animals. So not only do we waste energy transporting food to our tables, we waste resources creating chemicals used in raising the food itself.

In addition, the time lag between harvesting food and eating it gobbles up other resources. They are needed to keep food fresh longer while it is stored and shipped, often in refrigerated vehicles.

Fuel for Heating and Cooling

The building style and the location of cities and their suburbs also contribute to wasting resources. To get an idea of how this works, think about how much warmer you are when huddled together with a group of people. This same principle holds true for buildings.

In suburbia, the homes are usually built separate from one another, with space all around them and space between houses. These detached houses are exposed to weather on all sides. Many of them were built on open farmland, or surrounding trees were cut down so that the owner wouldn't have to rake leaves in the autumn. These factors make houses hard to heat in the winter, so they use more energy.

FACT

Heating a single-family home in winter and cooling it in summer account for 70 percent of the energy used in the American home. The refrigerator accounts for the next highest amount of energy used.

As land near cities becomes harder to find, more apartment buildings are being built in suburbs. Apartments and attached homes are cheaper to heat because they share walls and ceilings and floors, so less heat is lost to the outside.

Although the closeness of buildings in the city keeps them warmer in the winter, it may also keep them warmer in the summer. By sharing walls, ceilings, and floors, high-rises have less surface exposed to the hot summer sun. However, groups of tall buildings with very little greenery around them create "heat islands" that keep cities warmer in summer. Congested traffic burns oil, releasing more heat into the air. As a result, busy downtown areas use more energy to air-condition apartments, stores, and offices.

Contrast this with the buildings in smaller tropical and desert cities designed before energy became cheap and widely available. They remained cool in summer because they were built with wide shadowy porches that kept direct sun out of windows. Many stood on stilts or posts to let cool breezes flow under and around them. In especially hot deserts, heavy adobe or stone houses were built attached to one another around shaded courtyards.

Unfortunately, tightly packed skyscrapers now dominate city architecture throughout the world.

The Acoma Pueblo in New Mexico has been inhabited since A.D. 600. The adobe homes have thick, common walls and are repaired—not demolished—as needed.

Wasting Water

Next to air, water is our most important resource. Without water, humans would survive only a few days. Our bodies are two-thirds water, and it must continuously be replenished. We need it to drink, to keep ourselves clean, and to water

our plants and our animals. Water is fun, too—to swim in, boat on, splash around in, and just look at. But many areas of the world are running out of water already, including parts of North America, Africa, China, the Soviet republics, and India.

FACT

Including water used by industry and agriculture, as well as personal use, Americans use 580,000 gallons (2,204,000 liters) per person each year. Americans use 4 times as much as in Switzerland, and 70 times the amount used in Ghana. Most water goes to large, factory-like farms, created to feed city people.

Agriculture alone uses 85 percent of all water, with 50 percent used to raise animals, especially cows, for meat. (It's not that the animals drink so much, but the grain they eat requires water to grow.) Raising food takes seven times as much water as we use for washing and drinking.

Water is being taken from underground reservoirs called aquifers faster than it can be replenished by rain. It's no wonder that beneath one-quarter of the irrigated land in the United States, the level of the groundwater is sinking up to 4 feet (1.2 meters) per year! The deeper our water table sinks, the more it costs to get the water. We may not have enough water to go around within 10 or 20 years.

Today's cities and suburbs are contributing to this future catastrophe. For example, our pampered lawns use more water than the natural landscape, and most of the plants— grass, flowers, shrubs—may be good to look at, but are not very useful. They don't supply food for us or for animals.

They just use up water and human energy.

The sprawl that Los Angeles has become sits in the middle of a desert. To water their lawns and fill their swimming pools, Angelenos have their water transported from 300 to 400 miles (480 to 640 kilometers) away. In 1991, when a drought had lasted several years, water was tightly rationed. The lawns were the first things to go.

As cities the world over expand, more and more land is paved over. That causes water to be wasted, too. Pavement prevents rainwater from soaking into the ground. Instead, it goes into sewers, and eventually into rivers, bays, and oceans. We can't use it, and it doesn't replenish the Earth.

As the Southern California drought continued on into the 1990s, many people questioned the benefits of unchecked urban growth.

Losing the Land

You may not think of the ground beneath your feet as a resource, but without it, very few plants would grow. Topsoil—the upper and most fertile layer—is a special concern to environmentalists.

We are losing our land resources at a dizzying rate by covering it up and by washing it away. Two-thirds of the area covered by downtown Los Angeles, California; Phoenix, Arizona; and other especially car-dependent cities, is not used for people. It's reserved for cars in the form of roads, parking lots, and service stations. That's true of half the land in the average North American city.

Valuable natural resources are lost to urban growth. In Third World countries, deforestation is increasing. Most of these bags of charcoal (left), made from trees felled in a Costa Rican forest, will end up in cities for fuel. In North America, millions of acres of farmland are paved for roads and parking lots (right).

Disneyland, an amusement park in Anaheim, California, is as big as a small town. The park itself covers 77 acres (31 hectares), but its parking lot is even bigger—106 acres (43 hectares) is paved over just for cars!

City sprawl, suburban housing developments, and shopping centers have covered over the good farmland. Farmers are forced to move their crops onto the slopes and poor soils left over. Because the soil is poor, farmers rely on chemicals to coax the land to produce. These chemicals get washed into the groundwater, adding to the pollution problem.

Every year, as world population grows, we need to feed 93 million more people, but we lose 24 billion tons (21.7 billion metric tons) of topsoil by development and erosion.

FACT

Since 1967 the United States has paved over more farmland than the area of New Hampshire, Vermont, Massachusetts, Connecticut, and New Jersey combined. Each year we lose another 3 million acres (1.2 million hectares) of farmland to suburban sprawl. There are 3 million miles (4.8 million kilometers) of paved roads, which, along with parking lots, add up to 10 percent of the land that is fit for cultivation.

Wasting the Lives of People

People are a resource, too. And both industrialized cities and Third World cities waste human lives in ways that are sometimes similar, and sometimes different.

Cars versus Lives. The dependence of people in industrial nations on cars wastes time and money and causes a lot of suffering. The most obvious and direct way that cities dependent on cars waste the lives of people is by killing them.

Over a quarter of a million people die each year in car accidents around the world. That's twice as many people as were killed by the atomic bombs dropped on Hiroshima and Nagasaki, Japan, to end World War II. Every year in the United States alone, 50,000 people die in car accidents.

FACT

In the United States, cars had killed 1 million people by 1952, 2 million by 1975, and by the mid-1990s, 3 million will have died. More Americans have died in car accidents than were killed in all the wars since 1776.

In addition, 10 million people are injured in auto accidents, leaving some permanently disabled and even paralyzed. No wonder the automobile has been called the most destructive machine ever invented!

Another way car-dependent cities and suburbs waste our lives is by taking up a lot of our time. In Los Angeles, for example, commuters spend three to four hours a day sitting in cars that barely move during the "rush" hour. Americans will lose about 8 billion hours stuck in traffic by the year 2005.

Driving and owning a car may not seem cheap to you or your parents, but cars would be even more expensive without government support. You may not realize it, but cars are subsidized (partly paid for) by the government in many ways that make it seem cheaper to drive than it really is. Our taxes pay the wages of police officers and highway patrol to control traffic, and they buy and maintain highway lighting, signs, and signals.

In Europe, where gas is taxed much more heavily than it is in the United States, gasoline costs about $3 to $4 per gallon (3.8 liters). A much higher proportion of their gasoline tax goes to mass transit. Gas seems cheap in America, but if you include the costs to the environment and the cost of defending our access to foreign oil, gas costs nearly $18 per gallon.

Not only the United States is suffering. Canada recently reduced its railroad support by half. The only long-distance train that went between major cities all the way across the continent was shut down in 1990. Even Europe, which has many excellent railroads, is reducing service on some lines. But they are also bringing more high-speed lines into service.

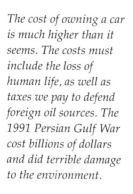

The cost of owning a car is much higher than it seems. The costs must include the loss of human life, as well as taxes we pay to defend foreign oil sources. The 1991 Persian Gulf War cost billions of dollars and did terrible damage to the environment.

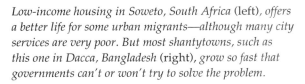

Low-income housing in Soweto, South Africa (left), *offers a better life for some urban migrants—although many city services are very poor. But most shantytowns, such as this one in Dacca, Bangladesh* (right), *grow so fast that governments can't or won't try to solve the problem.*

Wasted Lives in Shantytowns. The Third World cities waste human lives with cars, but they also waste them by ignoring the lives of the people in the shantytowns. For decades, the officials in such cities have regarded the residents of the "temporary" shantytowns as intruders who had no business being there. Occasionally they built low-income housing for migrants, but for each person who moved out of these shack slums, two more moved in from the country. In many cities, there are more people in the shantytowns than in the actual city. But still these people and the potential energy they can offer to the country are ignored. Sometimes they're not even counted in the official census of population.

No one knows for sure just how many people live in the shantytowns of Third World cities. What is certain is that human lives are being wasted by the urban environment they live in. They breathe polluted air, they drink polluted water, they fail to get an education . . . but still they hope.

Chapter 4

Today's Cities
Pollute Our Planet

HUMAN BEINGS AND ALL FORMS OF LIFE create waste products every second of every day. Every time you breathe, you exhale carbon dioxide and other wastes your body has created. Every time you eat or drink, the parts your body doesn't use turn into waste.

Fortunately, what one creature produces as waste is often usable by another. Your exhaled carbon dioxide is breathed in by plants; their waste product, oxygen, is what we breathe to survive. Many such cycles exist in nature, keeping things in balance.

Our Earth has a wonderful capacity to use waste and to cleanse itself. But today we are creating too much waste, and creating it too fast, for the Earth's natural systems to handle. In addition, modern technology is creating substances that nature cannot turn into harmless or helpful substances.

Where Does Pollution Come From?

Our sprawling suburbs and our city life are a major source of pollution in the air, water, and soil. The resources we waste most—fossil fuels—are a major source of pollution. These fuels pollute all along the way: when we look for them, extract them, process them, transport them, and finally when we burn them.

North Americans generate more garbage than any other people in the world. About 1,460 pounds (662 kilograms) of trash is thrown away each year for each Canadian, and 1,300 pounds (590 kilograms) for each American.

FACT

Today's city life and waste-collection practices reinforce the "throw-away society" of developed nations—we just toss out many things that are broken or worn and buy new ones, rather than getting the old ones fixed. We buy food and other items wrapped in more packaging than is really needed. That packaging is instant garbage.

Disposing of Garbage. North American cities usually handle trash in one of two ways: dumping in landfills (special holes in the ground) or incineration (burning). Both of these methods have many drawbacks, including pollution.

Most of our trash ends up in landfills. They are special areas that have hard clay or plastic on the bottom. Trash is dumped on top, with soil spread over it. Week after week, year after year, more trash and more soil are added until the whole thing is covered up.

Landfills take up space, and we are steadily running out of space near cities. As landfills fill up and close down, more and more cities truck their garbage farther away, using more fuel and costing more money.

Edmonton, Alberta, a city of 785,000 people, realized in the 1980s that it had a serious problem—municipal waste. The people knew that the landfill they used would be full by

This landfill in New York is filling up. The amount of garbage that must be disposed of is growing even faster than the population.

1991, so they tried to find a new location to dump the waste. After nine years and $3 million in expenses, they still couldn't get approval on a site. Through the efforts of many people, recycling became the "in" thing in Edmonton. The city has finally found a new landfill site, but they hope, through recycling, that Edmonton will never again need to look for another landfill.

Landfills also leak chemicals into our drinking water. According to the Environmental Protection Agency, less than one-third of our toxic-waste dumps are built to keep poisons in hazardous waste from our underground water supplies.

Incineration, once thought to be the answer to our growing garbage-disposal problem, is not the perfect alternative. Burning waste releases gases that pollute the atmosphere. It also leaves behind ash, which can contain toxic substances. When the ash is buried, the toxics can leak into the ground, eventually reaching our drinking water and our oceans.

Many North American cities have started recycling waste as one of the ways to handle the increasing amount of municipal waste.

Waste in Developing Nations. The developing nations do not produce as much waste as the developed nations because the people do not buy and use as many things. In addition, they had a tradition of reusing and recycling long before it became a popular thing to do in developed nations. In fact, many people in shantytowns make their living by scavenging through garbage for anything that might be usable or salable for recycling.

Mexico City has more money available to the residents than there is in most other developing nations, and they spend it on the same kind of consumer goods as residents of Montreal or Chicago. They buy fast foods in Styrofoam containers, plastic items that easily break, products that come in far too much packaging. They "consume like a first-class industrial power," said one observer.

When Mexico City's population starting growing so fantastically in the 1960s, it had never established a system for handling waste. And since then there has been neither the time nor the money to put one in place. So garbage mounts up in dumps wherever space can be found.

Shantytown residents often live right by the dumps. They scavenge through the garbage, hoping to find items that people will buy from them for recycling—bottles, rags, plastic containers. These garbage pickers also collect food waste to feed the pigs they keep.

Uncollected garbage often piles up beside Mexico City streets even though the city has built a huge landfill.

The city has built one mammoth landfill that is supposed to replace all the smaller dumps, but no plan has been made for replacing all the recycling that has been done by the shantytown garbage pickers.

Cairo, Egypt; Bombay, India; and many other Third World cities rely heavily on poverty-stricken residents to pick through the garbage and find things for recycling. It provides them with an income and limits the amount of waste that the city must actually find a place for.

50

Pollution from Growing Things. The way we grow our food and other plants also creates pollution. Huge corporate farms—and even not-so-huge ones—have become dependent on chemicals that end up in our air, soil, and water. Farmers have been pouring 2 billion pounds (0.9 billion kilograms) of artificial pesticides on our land every year, plus additional chemicals in fertilizers and herbicides.

Fortunately, our farmers are beginning to use organic, non-chemical, methods. But now farmers in Third World countries are beginning to use more fertilizers, hoping to improve the productivity of their poor soil.

Suburbanites use 3 to 6 times more pesticides per acre (0.4 hectare) on their lawns than farmers use on their crops! In 1990 Americans spent an incredible amount of money—$6.4 billion—on products such as pesticides, herbicides, and fertilizers. Much of them end up polluting the environment.

FACT

"Urban Soup"—Air Pollution

Can anything be more important than the air we breathe? We need it, animals need it, plants need it—we all need it to live, to survive. Yet we are dirtying it and changing its composition at an incredible rate. What gets into our air also frequently gets into our water and soil.

One hundred years ago, most air pollution was caused by the coal that fueled the Industrial Revolution. Burning coal is still a major pollution source in such places as Eastern Europe and China. However, cars and industries are now the main culprits in more industrialized areas.

FACT

Many air-pollution problems—smog, global warming, and acid rain—stem from overuse of fossil fuels. Twenty years after the federal government passed a Clean Air Act, more than 100 U.S. cities still do not meet clean-air standards. In 1988, 150 million Americans lived in areas that had unhealthy levels of air pollution.

Air pollution causes smog to form—that hazy, brownish, smelly stuff that hangs in the air and makes your eyes hurt and tear, and makes it hard to breathe, too. Cars are responsible for 50 percent of the hydrocarbons and nitrogen oxides that lead to smog, and 80 percent of the carbon monoxide.

Mexico City is one of the most unhealthy cities in the world. Children and old people must stay inside many days each year because of air pollution.

Mexico City. Mexico City has more than 22 million people. The city has about 6 million cars. Also, the industries burn coal high in sulfur, which pollutes the air. The city is located in a valley so low that winds do not often blow through it to clear pollution.

Since 1989, some major changes have been made that will help the environment.

Mexico City passed a law requiring that every car be left at home one workday each week. That day is determined by the license number. (However, the wealthy people are buying extra cars to use on the days when they aren't supposed to drive.) In addition, the city is replacing, as quickly as possible, its 12,000 minibuses with models that use unleaded gasoline. The taxi cabs (40,000 of them!) must have catalytic converters installed to limit air pollution. Some factories, especially metal foundries and an oil refinery in the suburbs, are being shut down. Mexico City is taking some actions before the problems get even worse.

Always on the Go

How far does your family travel every day? Walk or ride your bike to each place. If you don't have an odometer (an instrument that measures distance) to attach to your ankle or bike, calculate the mileage by counting the blocks. Usually 12 city blocks is equal to 1 mile (1.6 kilometers).

What is the round-trip distance to the grocery store, post office, theater, school, library, video shop, etc.? How often do you go to each location weekly? How do you go—walk, bicycle, light rail, bus, or car? How far do your parent(s) travel to work?

Keep records for one week on all members of your family and their mode of travel. If the week was typical, multiply the total by 52 to get an annual estimate.

Work out a plan to reduce this figure. Walk or bike all you want. Ride the bus instead of using the car. Make a list of things you need and shop once a week instead of daily.

Reducing travel saves fossil fuels and cuts down on pollution.

The Warming Earth—Greenhouse Gases. In the United States and Canada, pollution from cars is the biggest source of gases that are warming our Earth and changing our climate. Cars alone spew out nearly one-third of the excess carbon dioxide, the main culprit. Other troublesome gases are nitrogen oxide and methane (created by burning fossil fuels) and chlorofluorocarbons (CFCs), used in aerosol spray cans and air conditioners and in making Styrofoam.

These gases are called "greenhouse" gases because when they are released into the atmosphere, they act like the glass in a greenhouse. They allow the energy of the sun to pass through and trap a certain amount of it as heat. Without this *greenhouse effect,* our world would be icy and uninhabitable.

For centuries, the greenhouse effect kept our planet's temperature in balance. Now there's evidence that the balance is shifting, that greenhouse gases are building up, trapping more heat, and raising the planet's temperature. This is called *global warming.*

If global temperatures rise as much as some scientists predict, it could spell disaster by the middle of the next century. There could be less rain and snow in some areas, causing crops to fail and deserts to expand. In other areas, rain could increase and cause floods. Many plants and animals would have to shift their habitats or die out. Sea levels would rise, wiping out coastal areas and contaminating groundwater with salt.

For the first time in history humans have played a role in changing climate. The change we are now seeing may be occurring faster than we can adapt to it. Global warming could cause widespread suffering for many of Earth's inhabitants, all because we are hooked on fossil fuels.

The Thinning Ozone Layer. Air pollution from today's cities is also contributing to the thinning of our ozone layer. Ozone is a gas that is bad for us when it's down near the ground and good when it's up in the stratosphere, the upper atmosphere. In the stratosphere, ozone collects in a layer that protects all living things from getting too much of the sun's harmful ultraviolet rays.

Scientists have discovered that the ozone layer is becoming thinner all over the planet. CFCs and other artificial chemicals are destroying ozone, molecule by molecule. Some sources of CFCs have already been stopped, but no replacement for those used in cars has yet been found. And the CFCs that are already in the stratosphere will continue doing their damage for 75 years or more. We have no idea how to get rid of them.

A study of the movement of halocarbons—relatives of CFCs—from Los Angeles show that they have traveled into the deserts of Nevada and Arizona. They are accompanied by smog, which settles into the Grand Canyon. If residents of Los Angeles drive eastward on a vacation, they run into their own polluted air.

FACT

Acid Rain. Acid rain is another major environmental problem related to air pollution from cities. Acid rain (really acid *precipitation* because it includes acid snow, acid fog, and acid dew) consists mainly of sulfuric acid and nitric acid. Sulfur dioxide and nitrogen dioxide are released into the atmosphere by burning fossil fuels. Once there, they combine with water and turn into acids. Car exhaust emits one-third of the nitrogen dioxide contributing to acid rain.

Wind currents can carry sulfur and nitrogen oxides for hundreds of miles. So one country's or state's acid precipitation is often caused by another region's air pollution. This is the case in Canada, where half the acid rain comes from U.S. power plants and factories.

Acid rain has been found in many parts of the world, especially Europe, Japan, Canada, and the United States. For example, rain in the eastern United States is about as acidic as tomato juice! In southern California, fog may be 1,000 to 2,000 times more acidic than normal.

Acid rain makes lakes and streams more acidic, so fish have trouble reproducing and eventually die out. It makes algae grow too much, blocking out sunlight and oxygen from other plants and animals. It damages trees and crops by ruining the soil they grow on and weakening the trees.

Water Pollution

Humans began polluting Earth's water when they started dumping garbage and human wastes into rivers and lakes. Water, it seemed, just washed everything out of sight, or diluted it so it was no longer unpleasant. It seemed dilution was the solution.

In bygone days, bacteria were the problem. Dirty water bred bacteria and other germs, which spread disease. But, even if people polluted surface water this way, they still had clean groundwater to drink and use.

Today, our groundwater is becoming contaminated, too. And the biggest danger for our drinking water is not disease-spreading bacteria but poisonous chemicals.

India's Ganges River is one of the most polluted rivers in the world. And yet many people still bathe in the river as part of a religious ritual.

One source of pollution is urban runoff. Every time it rains, the water carries any waste material on the street along with it. Paved city streets and highways are covered with waste—oil, gasoline, lead from air pollution, asbestos from brake linings—most of which comes from cars. Rain washes this unappetizing mixture down into our groundwater or into our lakes and rivers.

The Cuyahoga River in Ohio was used for a hundred years or more as the dumping ground for the cities of Cleveland and Akron. It was also a source of drinking water. In the late 1960s, before people realized what they had been doing, the river was so polluted that it frequently caught on fire.

FACT

Many cities obtain their drinking water from groundwater sources. As far back as 1980, the New York Public Interest Research Group found that major aquifers (underground pools of water) under Long Island were seriously contaminated with waste, a lot of which came from highway runoff. Other aquifers are sinking so fast from overuse that the cost of pumping the water is now too high.

According to consumer advocate Ralph Nader, the drinking water in the United States contains more than 2,100 *different* toxic chemicals.

The Mississippi River is the source of drinking water for millions of people. Yet many areas of it have been closed to swimming and fishing because of pollution. It is possible that high rates of cancer reported in many cities are related to the drinking water supply. Many cities are dependent on

Because the public water supply in many Latin American cities is unsafe, some people buy bottled water. But people in slums and shantytowns who can't afford to purchase water often become ill or die from waterborne diseases such as dysentery and cholera.

bottled water for personal use. The people in New Orleans, Louisiana, buy the most bottled water of any U.S. city.

Pollution in the Oceans. Many of the world's largest cities are on water—oceans, lakes, rivers. If the water gets polluted, the cities suffer. On the other hand, the cities themselves pollute their water, often just by being there and having so many people.

We all hear about the larger oil spills. The *Exxon Valdez* spilled 11 million gallons (42 million liters) off the Alaskan coast in 1989. During the Persian Gulf War in 1991, Iraqi soldiers deliberately let millions of gallons of oil run into the gulf. The drinking-water supplies of cities along the desert coast were endangered when the oil neared the desalination plants that convert seawater to fresh water.

These big spills get the headlines, but a greater problem is the many, many little spills that we don't hear about. They add up to a major pollution problem. Twenty *Exxon Valdez*-sized oil spills of used motor oil are carelessly dumped by do-it-yourself mechanics each year!

Oceans and lakes are also polluted in other ways. Today, about 40 trillion pounds (18.14 trillion kilograms) of waste enter our oceans every year—about 80 percent of it from city sewage, industrial waste, and agricultural runoff. Our cities have long dumped untreated sewage, solid garbage, and other wastes into nearby water. Ocean dumping of untreated sewage will be illegal after 1992.

FACT

Soil Pollution

Soil is sometimes called dirt, and dirt is dirt, right? Who cares if it gets "dirtier"? Well, soil isn't just "dirt"—it's a mixture of all kinds of things—finely ground-up rocks and minerals, plus organic matter from decayed plants, worms, and insects. It took millions of years for it to be created by natural processes.

Topsoil (the most fertile layer of soil), like air and water, can become polluted with harmful substances. The pollution gets taken up by growing plants, and then passed on to animals, including us.

Until recently, it was thought that these substances degraded (broke down into harmless substances) quickly. But soil scientists have found that pollutants take a long time to degrade. They can pollute the food we grow for ourselves and for the cattle we raise for food. They can also seep into the groundwater we drink and into streams where fish live.

Gasoline is a problem, too. The federal government has found that 372 million barrels of waste from oil drilling are regularly dumped into pits in the earth. This waste often contains toxic substances that contaminate farmland. In addition, underground gasoline storage tanks at service stations often leak—and the gasoline goes into the ground.

Once topsoil is contaminated, it's basically impossible to clean it. You could bake it, but that would cost up to $1,000 per cubic meter. Besides, it's not always easy to test the soil, so how do we know which soil even needs cleaning?

An Earth Experience

The Pollution Tests

Find out how dirty the air is in your city. Look at the buildings—if they look gray or black, they are probably coated with pollution. If you can find one that's being cleaned, you can see the contrast between its dirty surface and the original clean one. On some buildings and statues, you might see damage—flaking and tiny holes—caused by acid rain and other air pollution.

You can see how pollutants in dirty water and dirty soil get into our food and our bodies. Put some food coloring or ink into a glass of water. Stand a white flower or a stalk of celery in the water. The plant will absorb the colored water and change color. It's the same with pollution. Pollution in water, or pollution carried in water from polluted soil, is absorbed by the plant. When people and animals drink polluted water, or eat food that has absorbed pollution, they absorb the pollution, too.

Check on the noise pollution in your area. Sit outside for at least 10 minutes and listen to the sounds. What do you hear? Cars? Buses? Trucks? Police cars? Fire engine sirens? Birds? Leaves rustling in the breeze? People laughing? People yelling? Loud music from boom boxes? How many of them are natural sounds? How many are artificial? How do the sounds make you feel? Happy? Relaxed? Nervous? What would you rather hear?

Noise Pollution

Most of us don't think about noise as being a form of pollution. But in a sense, it is. There are all kinds of sounds in the world. When sound becomes unpleasant—so loud it hurts our ears or makes it hard to concentrate or to hear what people are saying—that's NOISE!

Human beings evolved in a quiet setting. We needed to hear small sounds because they might help us survive—the sound of a twig snapping could mean an enemy was nearby. Loud noises, such as erupting volcanoes, thunder, and avalanches, usually meant trouble.

City dwellers are bombarded by noise: car engines starting and running, tires screeching, horns blaring, sirens wailing, trucks rumbling, airplanes zooming, the rat-a-tat-tat of streets being repaired, and buildings being torn down.

Steven Halpern, a sound researcher, has studied the increased noise level in cities. He found that before World War I, a brass bell was loud enough to alert traffic to an emergency vehicle. In the 1930s, the bell was no longer loud enough and sirens had to be used. By 1964, the siren had to be at 88 decibels. (A decibel is a unit used to measure sound.) Now the cities are so noisy that a siren has to scream at 122 decibels to be heard.

FACT

Wouldn't it be better if we designed our cities so we didn't burn up so much fossil fuel and didn't pollute our air, water, and soil? Wouldn't it be better if we didn't live in places that are too noisy? That's possible, as we'll see in coming chapters.

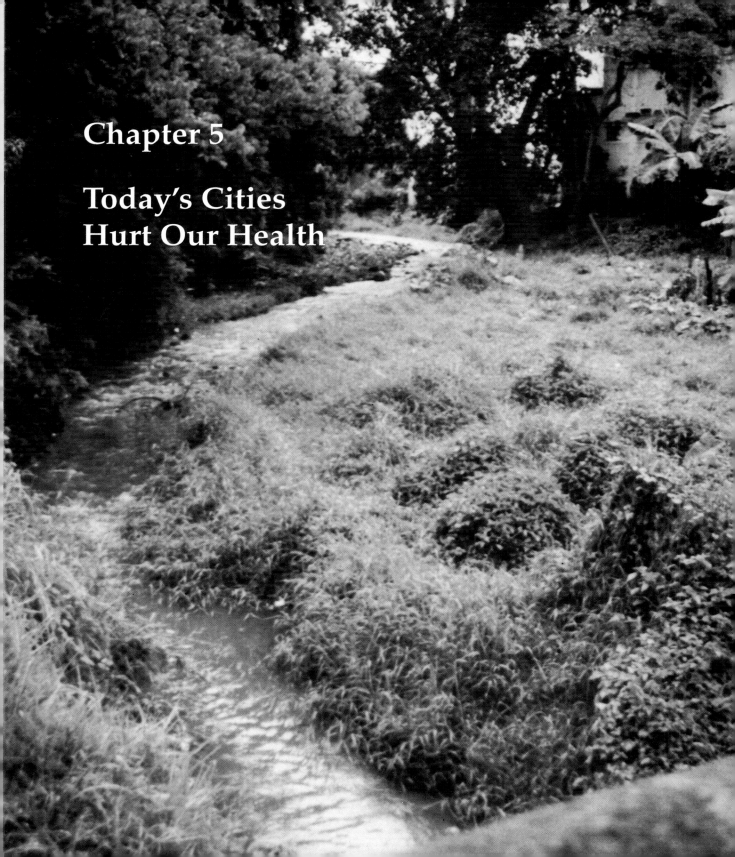

Chapter 5

Today's Cities
Hurt Our Health

AIR, WATER, AND SOIL POLLUTION are making cities increasingly unhealthy for people who live in them. But pollution is only a part of the picture. Car accidents kill and injure people, and urban stresses and tensions, especially driving in congested traffic, also affect our physical and mental health.

Poor people and members of minority groups who have no power suffer the most from the toxic products of urban life. They often live near freeways, dumps, or polluted waters, and work at jobs involving toxic substances. Their rundown neighborhoods are full of crime and drug abuse.

And in the Third World cities, all those problems and more combine to make life impossible for many people.

Life and Death in the Shantytowns

Every day 40,000 children in poor countries die of malnutrition and curable diseases. Most of them live in towns and cities that have little or no sewage systems, where their drinking water is contaminated with disease-causing germs. Jobs are few and transportation is poor.

Clean drinking water is often not available. Toilets may be nonexistent. The residents use whatever open areas they can find as their toilets—areas where children play and some people sleep. There is no garbage collection and no sewers, but there are rats. Tuberculosis, worms, influenza, dysentery, cholera, and typhoid can spread through a shantytown like wildfire, killing children and old people. Malnutrition kills more slowly but just as surely.

In such areas, whatever roads exist are often just open spaces between clumps of shacks. Children have

If a shantytown community is lucky, there might be a faucet set into the ground that is used by hundreds of people. Otherwise, they might get their water from a creek or a shallow well. In such a setting, disease may spread and bathing is impossible.

La Bolsa, the Mexican stock exchange (left), is a symbol of the wealthy few in Mexico City. Just one block away, shanties (right), built next to an eight-lane highway, indicate the poverty millions face each day.

few places other than those roads to play, and so they are killed by cars, too. Rarely do the children of the shantytowns go to school. Instead of learning to read, they learn to get money in any way they can, not always legally.

The World Health Organization has become increasingly concerned about life—and death—in the shantytowns. The fact that cities tend to have better health facilities than rural areas has nothing to do with the residents of the shantytowns. Health care isn't available to them. WHO officials are working with city leaders to make health concerns a major factor in plans for changing the cities.

Children the World Over

Young people seem to be more sensitive to pollution than adults. They breathe more air, drink more water, eat more food—and therefore take in more pollutants—for their size than do adults.

In addition, they have weaker defenses against harmful substances because their body's systems have not grown up and matured. They don't work quite like an adult's. Elderly people are also more at risk because their bodies are not working as well as they used to. But eventually everyone will be affected.

Breathing Becomes Difficult

You may have noticed that air pollution smells bad. It may sting your eyes and make them watery and itchy. It also may give you a headache and make you feel tired. Air pollution has become a major health problem in many cities all over the world. According to the United Nations, one-fifth of all people breathe air that is dangerously unhealthy.

In Athens, Greece, the death rate is six times higher on days when the air is heavily polluted. In Bombay, India, just breathing the air has the same bad effect on a person's health as smoking ten cigarettes a day. And in Los Angeles, there are days when the air is so bad that children are told to stay indoors.

Air pollution damages our respiratory, or breathing, system. It is the leading cause of such lung diseases as

Denver, Colorado, is surrounded by mountains that trap air pollution, turning the air into an unhealthy "brown cloud."

On a clear day in Los Angeles you can see for miles (left). *But most days the sky is filled with smog* (right) *that may make it hard to see farther than a block.*

emphysema, bronchitis, asthma, upper respiratory infections (colds and flu), sinus problems, and coughs.

Ozone, one of the most dangerous ingredients of smog, is created when sunlight interacts with pollutants called hydrocarbons and nitrogen oxides. Every time you inhale ozone, it damages your lungs. Your lungs can heal, but the damage leaves a scar that makes breathing more difficult.

A year after the record-high smog levels of the summer of 1988, Los Angeles doctors did an experiment. They examined the lungs of 100 young people who had died in accidents and from other non-health-related causes. They found that 80 of them had lung damage, and 27 of them suffered severe lung damage.

Smog also contains carbon monoxide, which is created during the burning of oil and gasoline. Special devices called catalytic converters in cars have reduced the amount of carbon monoxide released from cars by 90 percent, but there are countless millions of cars on the road, so they still create a lot of this gas.

Carbon monoxide is harmful because it combines with the hemoglobin in your blood—the part that carries oxygen—and prevents it from doing its job. When your cells don't get enough oxygen, you don't think as well, your reflexes get slower, and you may become sleepy. In some people, too much carbon monoxide can cause or worsen heart problems. And when pregnant women breathe carbon monoxide, it can affect their unborn babies.

In the city of Leipzig, in what was formerly East Germany, most heavy industry is powered by burning soft coal, which creates terrible, heavy smog. The residents of Leipzig live an average of six years less than the residents of the rest of that part of Germany because of respiratory problems related to air pollution.

FACT

Lead Poisoning. Cars and trucks also emit lead from the fuel they burn. Exposure to lead can permanently injure your brain. It can cause problems in hearing, talking, learning, and behavior. Children living near busy freeways may be exposed to a lot more lead than if they lived near a toxic-waste dump. Yet, we often build housing projects near freeways for people with low incomes.

Today, American gasoline contains much less lead than it used to. Nevertheless, one-third of the people living in North American and European cities still breathe air containing dangerous levels of lead.

Lead poisoning is considered the most common and worst environmental disease of young children. It affects 15 to 20 percent of urban children and 50 to 66 percent of inner-city children. And lead is not only in the air. Many inner-city children are harmed by swallowing paint chips from old, rundown buildings.

Once you get lead poisoning, its effects last forever. Lead poisoning is so damaging that California recently decided to test all its children for lead. They estimate that they will find 50,000 children each year who have too much lead in their bodies and may suffer permanent damage.

Food and Water

Today's cities, with their exploding populations, are dependent on huge farms run like food factories. And the farms have become dependent on chemicals, some of which are harmful. The toxic chemicals get into our air, water, and soil, ending up in the foods themselves.

Pesticides do more than kill unwanted pests. According to the EPA, pesticides in our food are one of our most serious health problems. Scientists have tested humans and other animals and found that probably all of us are walking collections of pesticides.

We're not sure what the presence of pesticides will do to the health of the average person, but we do know that the health of farmers, their families, and farm workers suffers from being around pesticides. The EPA estimates that 6,000 Americans, mostly farm workers, have cancer caused by pesticides. Yet, in spite of all these pesticides, we are losing

Many Americans in cities and suburbs apply large amounts of chemical pesticides to their lawns and gardens without realizing that the poisons end up in our food and water supply.

68

twice as many crops to insects as we lost before we used pesticides. People are starting to wonder if all these pesticides are really necessary.

But we can't blame all these pesticide-related illnesses on agriculture. People with lawns and gardens also use a tremendous amount of chemicals.

Unsafe Lawn Care. Chemicals sprayed on lawns evaporate into the air or wash off, and get into the land and water supplies. They can cause health problems for the whole community—and beyond. Although these chemicals, along with huge amounts of water, help keep our lawns green and free of weeds, they are poisons. They harm innocent bystanders such as useful bugs and earthworms, pets, songbirds, and people.

Pesticides used on suburban lawns can cause headaches, dizziness, eye problems, confusion, and permanent damage to the nervous system. Some contain cancer-causing chemicals. In 1987, it was found that children who lived in houses where pesticides were used regularly had 6 to 9 times more leukemia (a type of blood cancer) than other children.

Because unemployment is so high in Latin America, many women sell food, clothing, and items scavenged from garbage to make enough money to feed their large families.

Quality of Life

There's more to health than air, food, and water. The complete picture includes mental and emotional health: Are we happy? Do we like our lives? It includes social health: Do we have good relationships with other people? Are people treated fairly? It includes economic health: Can people find jobs that they like and that pay enough money to buy the things they need?

Life in today's cities is becoming more unpleasant and uncomfortable. In other words, the "quality of life" is not good. Neither our overcrowded city centers nor our spread-out suburbs supply everyone with a high quality of life.

Most people like to be close to other people, to be near friends, to share thoughts. We want to enjoy good times together and help each other through bad times. We like to talk and play and work together.

Stresses of Life in the City. On the other hand, having too many people around all the time is not fun. When people live under crowded conditions, many of them get uncomfortable. Buses and subways are too full. Lines at stores are too long. Classrooms are too crowded, and schools go on double sessions. People miss their privacy.

There may not be enough room to play, or relax, or just to live. Streets get dirtier and sometimes dangerous when too many people use them. There aren't enough fire fighters, police officers, or other services. Crime increases, housing gets too expensive. The city gets too noisy.

FACT

Some poor, inner-city areas of Chicago have more murders in them each weekend than take place in many entire countries. These mostly occur between members of rival gangs or in drug deals that go wrong. In 1991 the city averaged 71 murders each month. How can the people who live in such areas ever relax?

As the population of Third World cities increases, urban stress multiplies. Mexico City's growing traffic adds to unhealthy air pollution (top left). Dacca, Bangladesh (top right), doesn't have as many cars as Mexico City, but both cities are facing growing populations, unemployment, and spreading shantytowns. Supplying energy without pollution is also a problem for most cities. This African power plant (bottom right) is a major polluter. Adequate housing is a worldwide dilemma; these homeless children on the outskirts of Jakarta, Indonesia (bottom left), may never have homes.

71

Living in such conditions can cause stress and make people unhappy. It can make us angry—we may say and do nasty things. It can make us feel depressed, and interfere with our sleep, and our concentration. Too much stress can eventually cause high blood pressure, muscle aches, headaches, poor digestion, fatigue, heart disease, and lowered resistance to other diseases.

Suburbs Can Be Stressful, Too. Suburban life isn't for everyone either. We might feel hassled and nervous in the overcrowded city, but people can feel very lonely living in the spread-out suburbs. It's hard to visit other people when they live so far away and you need a car to travel.

Some people find suburbs boring—and boredom creates its own kind of problems. Suburbs don't always have low crime rates either. Sometimes, crimes—robbing, destroying property, fighting, abusing drugs—are committed just for excitement. And since many suburbs are deserted during the day while people are at work, it's easier for people to get away with breaking the law.

Many parents are so busy commuting and working to pay for housing, cars, and better schools, that they have very little time to spend with their kids. They worry about whether their kids are all right, if they are safe, especially if they are "latchkey" children who stay home alone after school. And parents who can afford to pay for child care worry if that care is good enough.

A lot of these stresses are due to cities and suburbs being so car-oriented. Have you ever noticed how people get nervous and crabby when they are stuck in traffic? What happens when someone cuts them off or they miss a turn-off? What if traffic makes a driver late for work or late in picking up a child from school? That might make people take chances that they ordinarily wouldn't.

Hearing loss can happen very gradually when a person is exposed to loud noises over a long period of time. Continuous noise at levels above 70 decibels can cause deafness. Diesel truck noise is about 82 decibels. Heavy city traffic is about 90.

FACT

Cities and Exercise. Driving everywhere, rather than walking or riding a bike, means we get less exercise. Human beings just aren't meant to be sitting around all day. It makes us lazy and sluggish. It robs us of energy, weakens our muscles and bones, and leaves us more likely to get sick. And it makes us fat. In fact, studies show that the more TV kids watch, the more overweight they are.

San Francisco is a leader in developing auto-free bike paths so that city residents can travel almost anywhere in the city without driving a car.

Some of us try to get around this by going to a health club or gym. We spend lots of money and time sweating and burning calories to lose weight and stay in shape. But wouldn't it make more sense if we could bike or walk to school or work? If we could play more games outside? If there were nearby trails to hike?

Designing car-dependent cities is unfair to those people who can't afford cars and can't travel easily, if at all. They can't enjoy nice places or visit people.

73

They may have trouble getting to work. Their quality of life is much lower than it would be if cities were designed for people—all the people—and not for cars.

Healthy Communities

The World Health Organization (WHO) has developed demonstration projects for healthy cities. The first twelve included Copenhagen, Denmark; Zagreb, Yugoslavia; and Liverpool, England. Now there is a network of hundreds of communities in Europe.

The concept has spread from Europe to Australia, New Zealand, Canada, and the United States. In America the effort is called the Healthy Communities Project and in-

Copenhagen, Denmark, was one of the first cities to join the Healthy Cities Program. The Danish government supported the establishment of electric railways and an efficient bus system for suburbanites who have to commute. Large areas of open space also make city life more enjoyable.

Indianapolis, Indiana, has become more environmentally aware since becoming a "healthy city." Soon all city parks will be connected by bicycle and walking paths. And the idea of eliminating downtown car traffic is gaining in popularity.

cludes twenty cities such as Indianapolis, Indiana; Boston, Massachusetts; and Pasadena, California.

The Healthy Communities Project is tied to a program called Healthy People 2000. The planners are certain that the health of all Americans can be improved by making major changes in the urban environment. One such change would be to create places in each neighborhood where people could exercise in pleasant surroundings. Another would be to treat waste with biological processes instead of chemical. It's possible that the program may eventually succeed in eliminating motor vehicles in crowded downtown areas.

Sherbrooke, Quebec, a Canadian city of 150,000 people, was planning to hire more police to keep gangs and drug dealers out of their abandoned downtown. The Canadian Healthy Communities Project helped the city make different plans. The parking meters were removed so that enough parking was available. The littered, filthy streets were swept and cleaned each Wednesday night. The abandoned school was turned into a counseling and activity center for young people. Trees were planted, creeks cleaned up, and toxic trash removed. Sherbrooke's businessmen encouraged shops to return to the downtown area, and the city center came back to life, because its citizens cared.

Chapter 6

Today's Cities Hurt Nature

IN THE PAST, HUMANS WIPED OUT, or nearly wiped out, some species of animals through hunting. Animals were hunted for food and clothing, and in some cases, just for "fun." The American buffalo, or bison, is just one example. These huge, dark beasts were so plentiful that they turned the prairies to what some explorers called "seas of black." As recently as the mid-1800s, about 60 million bison roamed the Great Plains. Now, there are no more wild bison in the United States. A few small herds exist in reserves.

In addition, all through history many cities and communities cut down too many trees for fuel and buildings. They completely destroyed the nearby forests. All over the world, we still hunt animals for food, chop down forests for wood, and clear land for agriculture and cattle.

But suburban sprawl and urban-related pollution may prove to be more deadly for wild animals and plants than the shotgun, the fishing net, and the axe. Today's expanding cities are taking more and more of the land where only wild plants and animals used to live. As a result, urban development and pollution are making a big contribution to the loss of plants and animals.

Leonard Duhl, a University of California professor, says, "We cannot save our natural environment and open space unless we save our urbanized spaces."

Some scientists think that as many as 17,500 plant and animal species become extinct each year—about 50 a day! They predict that as cities grow and forests are cut down to support them, we could soon lose several hundred species each day.

FACT

Shrinking Habitats—There's No Place Like Home

Animals can't live just anywhere—they need a special home, or habitat, that provides them with the food, shelter, and space they need.

Any time we build over land, we take away some of the habitat that belonged to plants and animals. Sprawling cities take up much more land than compact cities, and so are much more harmful to the natural environment. Every time another spread-out urban housing development is built, or an industrial park, shopping mall, a road or parking lot—every time we pave over the land, more plants and animals lose their habitats.

Wet, But No Longer Wild

Over 80 percent of the wetlands surrounding Canada's large cities have been lost to urban expansion and agriculture. The wetland on the left is now a farm. Homes and suburbs (right) are quickly moving in to displace it and the remaining wildlife.

Did you know that thousands of miles of creeks, streams, and rivers now flow in concrete channels under the ground? How did this happen? As our cities were built, some people decided creeks were inconveniently placed. So they buried or re-routed them to get them out of the way.

In some cases, this was almost understandable. People had been dumping garbage in creeks, so they came to be thought of as dirty places. It was no great loss—in fact, it became an advantage to bury them.

When a creek or stream is polluted this way, most of its wildlife disappears. Animals living near the creek, such as birds, also suffer, since they depend on waterways for food and drinking water.

In addition, we dam up our rivers, and drown beautiful valleys to supply water and water power to cities and farms. Not only do habitats disappear, but aquatic animals get sucked into water pumps.

Urban development has also covered up wetlands. Wetlands—marshes, swamps, and bogs that are saturated with water at certain times of the year—support water-loving plants and animals. In the United States, 95 percent of the wetlands are inland, but some lie along the seacoasts. In Canada, more than three-quarters of the wetlands in populated provinces have disappeared.

For a long time, we thought of wetlands as wastelands—swamps filled with mosquitoes or snakes or other creepy critters. We thought it was a good idea to get rid of them. We are beginning to realize how valuable wetlands are.

Wetlands provide homes for millions of wildlife creatures. They also act like giant natural sponges. During heavy rainfall, they soak up the extra water and protect our homes from floods. In many cities located along rivers, flooding in the spring is worse today because the wetlands along the rivers have been paved over.

Wetlands act as natural filters, cleaning up the polluted water that runs off oily city streets and highways, as well as farmland where pesticides and fertilizer have been used. As a result, they make drinking and swimming water safe for us as well as for fish and other wildlife. Fish and water fowl reproduce and raise their young in coastal wetlands.

Jamaica Bay National Wildlife Refuge—between Brooklyn and Queens, New York—is an important migratory stop for shorebirds. This urban wetland is being polluted by storm-water runoff from city streets and Kennedy International Airport.

Animals on the Move

Animals move for many reasons—just like us. They move to find food, to find shelter, to find mates, to give birth. Some move daily, others migrate with the seasons. But human development is preventing animals from moving safely, and in some cases, preventing them from moving at all.

We have tried to save wilderness areas and protect habitats by creating special parks and wildlife refuges for animals to live. But these areas are more like island prisons for many animals. They are cut off from their migration routes and their usual home range by roads, fences, dams, suburban developments, and agricultural fields.

We're now learning that these man-made ecological islands are too small to support many plants and animals. In addition, there isn't a big enough population for mating animals to have a wide choice, so they all become too closely related, which can weaken a group of animals. And animals can't move across land taken over by humans. An estimated 100 million wild animals are killed each year by cars and trucks on America's roads.

City Pollution—Wildlife Death

Pollution from cities gets into water—rivers, lakes, bays, and oceans—and harms our health, but it harms animals and plants even more. Animals are harmed directly either by drinking the water or by swimming in it. Others are hurt by eating contaminated plants and smaller animals that live in polluted waters. Still others starve to death because pollution kills off plants and animals they depend on for food.

Oil is one of the biggest pollutants in harbor areas. It may be washed off the streets in runoff or continually poured into the water by industry. Whatever the cause, it can seriously damage the digestive systems of ducks and other birds, gradually causing them to starve to death. Or it coats and suffocates invertebrates on which larger animals feed. As oil-dependent cities and suburbs grow, the amount of oil being used, and spilled into waterways, will increase.

San Francisco Bay is being hurt because the fresh water that normally enters it is being diverted to farmland. Also, poisoned urban and agricultural runoff taint the water. The number of striped bass swimming in the bay has fallen by 85 percent over the last 20 years. More than 100,000 salmon used to pass through the bay during their winter run. Now the number is down to an almost nonexistent 300. Wildlife is threatened all over California, so the governor has declared a fish and wildlife emergency.

Europe's North Sea is on the verge of collapsing as an

Harbor seals (left) are on their way to extinction in the North Sea because pollution had weakened the seals' immune systems so they couldn't fight a virus epidemic. Oil spills both on land and water can kill animals of many different kinds. Here (right), a duck has been severely oiled. The oil will get into its digestive system when it preens its feathers.

ecosystem because of all the pollutants dumped into it. The incredibly long list includes waste from agriculture and industry, sewage, garbage, and runoff from cities; air pollutants from fossil fuels burned in car engines and power plants; and thousands of tons of spilled oil and toxic drilling mud from the North Sea oil fields.

In many Third World cities, garbage and other waste is still dumped in open heaps wherever there is room. These dumps are full of wildlife—birds, wild dogs, rats and other rodents. They are assured of finding things to eat in the barren city landscape.

Global Warming—Global Death

When looking at the ways that today's cities hurt nature, global warming has a huge potential for harm. Some experts say that if areas of Earth warm up by just a few degrees, it could pose a greater threat to wildlife than anything else we are doing to our environment.

Plants and animals evolved to live only in a certain temperature range. When the temperature changes, they must adapt, move to another place, or die. In the past, temperature changes happened slowly and trees and plants had time to migrate and adapt. But the increase in the greenhouse effect will force them to move ten times faster. If they don't, they will die out. Even if they could move that fast, how will trees and plants jump over cities and farmlands? And even if they do, how will the animals be able to migrate and follow their habitats?

In spite of these difficulties, some species of plants and animals will survive. But many will not. Scientists are worried that huge numbers of species will become extinct. For example, much of northern Canada and Alaska is covered with a vast forest that makes up 23 percent of the world's forests. As the temperature climbs and vegetation migrates from the south to the north, the cold-loving forest plants will have nowhere to go—there is no more land to the north.

Wetlands species will also suffer, and many will die. As sea level rises because of expansion of the warmer water, the coastlines will become submerged—taking up to 80 percent of American wetlands with them. Other wetlands in the center of the continent will dry up due to evaporation caused by higher temperatures.

Even animals and plants in "protected" areas such as national and state parks and wildlife preserves will be in trouble. We might be able to protect them from the loss of habitat due to direct effects of urban development, but not from the indirect effects such as global warming. Imagine coming home from school to find that your house has turned into a grass hut, with no water. Imagine having no refrigerator. And imagine that the supermarket carries only snake pies and alligator steaks. What would you do? What will the animals do if something like that happens to them? Will they survive?

Wildlife in the City

Collectors gather exotic plants and animals for people to put in their gardens and keep in their homes as pets. Some of these are illegally collected, and many are on the verge of becoming extinct. Even when living things are collected legally, the waste is incredible. One bird expert estimates that for every bird that shows up in a pet store, 100 may have died before they made it to the store. Wouldn't it be

Rats transmit many diseases such as tuberculosis that harm both humans and animals. One female Norway rat (above) can produce up to 100 offspring each year.

better to enjoy the wildlife that is native to our area—the animals that live in our cities?

Even though urban development is making the world a more difficult place for many animals to live in, there's more wildlife in cities than most of us think.

One of the most infamous inhabitants of cities is the rat. Actually, two main species of rats live in the same cities, and often in the same buildings. The black rat is about 8 inches (20 centimeters) long. It tends to live in dry places, eating everything it can find. The brown Norway rat—or sewer rat—tends to be a little larger and is often found in water. Both kinds of rats produce many young, so the rat population is in little danger of being reduced. That's unfortunate because they can carry diseases in their bites.

An Earth Experience

Is It Vacant?

People often look at a vacant lot as a place where nothing lives, a useless area that serves no purpose. However, it just may be the only place in town where wildlife can find a home.

Find a vacant lot in your neighborhood for an in-depth study. You will find it full of living things that have sought refuge from the concrete of the city. Here are some ideas to explore.

1. Walk through the area and identify the trees, shrubs, wild flowers, and grasses growing in it. Count the numbers of each. Which plants seem to dominate (have the most numbers)?

2. Take along an insect net and sweep the area with it. After you have identified what you catch, release them. They may be

Keeping everything clean and laying out poisons are about the only things that will clear a place of rats.

White-tailed deer are regarded as suburban deer because unlike most animals, they don't disappear as new suburbs grow. White-tails thrive on suburban garbage. There are more white-tailed deer in Canada and the United States now than there were when the first Europeans arrived.

Raccoons, opossums, woodchucks, skunks, and bats are common in the suburbs of North American cities. They frequently make their way into the hearts of the cities, though traffic usually kills them fairly quickly.

Other cities support more "exotic" animals. In Africa and Asia, storks, monkeys, large snakes, and even hyenas prowl city dumps. In India, cattle, sacred to the people, wander the streets, often causing traffic jams just by standing still.

---

needed to pollinate a flower or serve as food for larger animals that are struggling to survive in the urban environment.

3. Animals are difficult to count because they run for cover or fly away when humans come. Spend an hour sitting quietly by the vacant lot. Do any birds land? You may see a field mouse, ground squirrel, or rabbit scurrying around looking for breakfast. You will find anthills with the ants busily taking care of their chores.

4. Look for scats (the feces of animals). Books are available that teach you how to identify animals this way. You might see the droppings of an opossum, raccoon, or rabbit.

A vacant lot is a thriving community of plants and animals struggling to live in a human environment. If you think city life is hard for people, imagine what it is like for wildlife.

Certain birds also thrive in urban areas—pigeons, sparrows, gulls, and starlings seem to love city life. In fact, over 200 different kinds of birds live in New York City—and that's not counting the birds in the zoo! In addition, butterflies and other insects, lizards, raccoons, deer, foxes, squirrels, and even bears live in or sometimes visit our cities. Trees and other plants manage to survive in parks, empty lots, and backyards.

It's Not Easy Finding Green

Are you an environmentalist? Most people would answer "yes." Most of us care about trees, flowers, birds, and animals. But many people don't get a chance to enjoy nature directly—by being in it, seeing it, touching it, smelling it, feeling it all around us.

Our cities are partly to blame. Suburban development has destroyed much wilderness. Crowded cities have few green areas and more gray—brick, concrete, and glass. It's hard to get close to nature when we have so little of it left.

Big, busy cities can be exciting and interesting to be in and look at. That's good for our health. But scientists have discovered that being in an environment that includes natural living things is good for our health, too.

Just as our ancestors evolved in a quieter world, we evolved in a more natural world. Our bodies and minds seem to need trees and grass and other living things to make us feel happy. Most people feel much more relaxed after spending time with nature—whether it's puttering around a backyard garden or swimming in a lake. Even hospital patients recover faster when they can look at trees outside their windows!

If our cities had more natural, open spaces such as parks and streams—and not so many buildings, paved streets, and cars—we would feel more connected with nature. If we were closer to farms, orchards, and waterways, we would understand where food comes from, and where our garbage goes. We would understand what we are losing by building our cities out of balance with nature, and maybe we would work harder to stop it.

In the middle of Manhattan, New York City, Central Park gives millions of people 840 acres (340 hectares) of "relief" from city stresses.

Chapter 7

Designing the Cities of Tomorrow

IT'S CLEAR THAT SOMETHING IS WRONG with most of today's cities. They waste resources; they pollute our air, our water, and our land; they're not good for our bodies, our minds, or our relationships with other people; and they hurt plants and animals.

What kind of future do we want? Should it include cities at all? We need to give thought to those places that more than half of the world's people call home.

It makes sense to work on our cities because, first of all, so many of them already exist. That's just as well because today there are so many people in the world that if we all lived in the country, there wouldn't *be* any country. The world would be one gigantic, sprawling suburb.

Besides, cities have a lot to offer. Some people talk about the "magic" of the city—its creative, lively people; its streets; its theaters, museums, and schools; its excitement and its thrilling pace. The *density* (number of people per acre) of a city makes it possible for people to learn from each other, to enjoy things together, and to work together.

Compact cities do less damage to the environment, per person, than suburbs do. People in cities live close together, using less land. And it is easier and more efficient to provide the services they need—garbage collection, mail delivery, police and fire protection, hospitals.

Cities are at the center of human life. They challenge our creativity. They make it more likely that everyone will be heard and treated more fairly. So cities can be the best and biggest tool to help us understand and take better care of the world and each other . . . if we improve the way they are designed.

FACT

In some South American cities, migrants from the same rural region or extended families may build a whole settlement almost overnight. These squatter-builders usually use land that is owned by the city. They plan roads and open places and assign tiny lots to families. Then they build their "houses" with whatever materials they can find as quickly as possible so that their urban "village" is a fact before the officials discover it.

Planned Cities

Most cities have just grown, but throughout history, leaders have decided to design and build new cities for various reasons. Washington, D.C., for example, was planned in an empty area between Maryland and Virginia to calm the divisions between North and South. It was laid out by a Frenchman named L'Enfant. Beijing, the capital of China, was designed and redesigned each time it was conquered over the centuries. Chicago, Illinois, was laid out after the Great Chicago Fire of 1872.

More recently, several nations have chosen to build completely new capital cities away from the large cities that already existed. Brazil started constructing the spectacular new capital of Brasília in the interior of the country, far away from the old coastal cities, in 1956.

The Indian city of Chandigarh at the foot of the Himalayas was also built in the 1950s, with the principal design being done by world-famous French architect Le Corbusier. Although the Indians had few cars at the time, Le Corbusier designed the city to function around a network of roads for car travel. But the city has many green spaces, and small,

For many years the spectacular new city of Brasília failed to attract people because it was too new to have things to do besides work. But that problem has been solved with time and today the city has a population of more than 2 million.

friendly neighborhoods. It now has about a million people. There are still few cars, but motorcycles and motorized rickshaws crowd the road system Le Corbusier designed.

In the 1930s, the Brazilian state of Goiâs built a new capital city called Goiânia to replace one that existed in a malaria-infested swamp. Today it has 2.5 million people. Nigeria and Tanzania are also building new capital cities. They are already developing shantytowns.

Chandigarh, India, is a modern preplanned city designed by the world-famous architect Le Corbusier. It has many green spaces and small neighborhoods. This building is the university auditorium.

Urban Ecology

The science of ecology deals with the connections between living creatures and the connection between creatures and their environment. Urban ecologists study the connections between a city and everything living in it and between a city and the larger environment that the city is a part of.

Urban ecologists believe that redesigning cities gives us a chance to get at root causes of our environmental problems. For example, we have seen how harmful it is to depend on gasoline-powered cars for transportation. One possible solution to the problem would be to switch to electric cars.

But this would affect only one aspect of the problem—air pollution. If we burned fossil fuel or used nuclear energy to create the electricity, we would just move the pollution from one place to another. Also, we would still have clogged highways and deaths due to traffic accidents. And, we would still use too much land for roads and parking.

A greater change would be for people to walk or take public transit. But this is not always practical or even possible, because sprawl spreads things too far apart to create good public transit or to walk to most places. A greater change would be to reduce the amount of sprawl—this would improve the air and help take care of other problems.

Redesigning our cities into *ecocities*—cities built on sound ecological principles—will make them better places to live. It will launch changes that reach far beyond the cities.

What's So Great About An Ecocity?

The ecocity will look to the future, but it will also improve the lives of people living today. Ecocities are better than today's cities because:

In an ecocity, residents work together to create clean cities. These teenagers in Salt Lake City, Utah, are part of a youth project to beautify rundown neighborhoods.

- Instead of wasting resources, the ecocity conserves them and emphasizes the use of renewable resources.
- Instead of polluting our air, water, and soil, the ecocity emphasizes the use of clean, nonpolluting energy sources in agriculture and other industries.
- Instead of hurting our health, the ecocity helps keep us healthy in body and mind.
- Instead of hurting nature, the ecocity exists in balance with nature and considers the needs of plants and other animals as well as those of humans.

Transportation Choices: Feet First

Because dependence on cars is at the root of so many urban problems, ecocities will be constructed so that most of us will get around by walking. When a place is too far to reach on foot, the ecocity offers transportation choices that are less harmful to the environment than cars.

In ecocities you will be able to get around easily and safely on bicycles (or skateboards or roller skates) and public transit. The public transit system might include buses, light-rail lines (like trolleys), ferries, and trains. They will be coordinated, with more frequent service, and with easy transfer between types of transportation. It will be safer, more affordable, and more convenient to use than cars.

Every full van that travels through a city removes 13 cars from the road. Every full bus removes 40 cars. Every full rail car removes 75 to 125 cars. If commuters used mass transit instead of private cars, they would put 90 percent less hydrocarbons and 75 percent less carbon monoxide and nitrogen oxide in the air.

Urban Density. To make it practical to get around without cars, ecocities will have a relatively higher density and a more compact layout, with much less space between buildings. When buildings are clustered close together, it's much easier to get around by walking.

Compact development may be clusters of small villages or neighborhoods. They may be commercial centers for shopping and for services such as doctors, hospitals, food shops, drug stores, movie theaters, video arcades, libraries and bookstores, day-care and senior centers, restaurants, snack shops, and shoe-repair shops.

Experts have calculated that it takes 16 people living on each acre (0.4 hectare) to get people out of their cars and make public transit practical. To make walking practical, there needs to be 40 people per acre.

San Francisco averages 23 people per acre and ranks third in density among cities in the United States. As a result, it has an excellent and well-used transit system and many people walk and bike from place to place. A study found that each time the density of the city doubles, car use in the San Francisco Bay Area is cut by 30 percent.

By comparison, Manhattan has a density of 104 people per acre. In most suburbs, the average is 2 to 8 people per acre—that's quite a difference.

How This Transformation Will Take Place. In areas where there are only houses and apartment buildings, such as many suburbs, businesses could be created by either adding new buildings or allowing stores to operate on the lower floors of multi-story residential buildings. In areas that contain only businesses, such as the downtown areas of big metropolitan cities, living spaces could be added above street-level businesses. This means that some cities could shrink and become more concentrated and less sprawled. Some could break up into smaller units.

We can also create compact cities along transit lines and concentrate centers of living or business close to transit stations. With shops right around transit stops, people could do their errands and then walk home.

The Sky's the Limit

In order to make cities denser, some of them will become more three-dimensional and have a variety of building heights. There could be more tall buildings—four, five, or six stories high—in lively city centers, where people both live and work.

What? No skyscrapers? Urban ecologists think there might be some, but very tall buildings cast big shadows and make cities dark. They require lots of people to be in one place at one time, but usually nothing is going on at ground level. Many skyscrapers are huge, ugly, high-rise boxes that make us feel small. And the way cities today are now built, big buildings increase automobile traffic.

But a tall building could make sense in an ecocity. If it were beautifully designed, if it were a mixed-use building, if there weren't too many others in the city—a tall building could save valuable land and add variety to the landscape.

Most urban ecologists point to the old cities of Europe, such as Paris and Rome, to give us an idea of the density and variety of building heights and sizes they feel would open up the crowded, congested, dark, uncomfortable-feeling metropolises of today.

It may be unrealistic to think we will ever reach the perfect balance of jobs, housing, and shopping in every single city so that no one would ever need a car. However, we can improve areas where these factors are way out of balance. All it takes is imagination and creativity. We created the car-dependent city fifty years ago. Now we can create cities that do not depend on cars!

Green and Open Space

Cities today were often built in ways that covered over or destroyed hills, creeks, shorelines, and open spaces. Ecocities will incorporate, preserve, and restore such natural and recreational resources.

Experts believe we need to establish a *greenbelt*—a housing-free zone around the cities to protect natural areas and farms. The greenbelt would have permanent boundaries within which no further development would be allowed. This would preserve existing habitats for migrating and permanent birds and other wildlife, as well as agricultural land, ranches, forests, recreation areas and parks, and wilderness areas.

The British Parliament established a 20-mile (32-kilometer) greenbelt around London in 1962. The area of 900 square miles (2,330 square kilometers) is very popular with residents.

96

Farms and Gardens. Greenbelts will include working farms, orchards, and ranches—all close to the city, so we could buy fresh produce at farmers' markets and community stores. Within the city, we could have vegetable gardens and ornamental gardens on rooftops, porches, patios, and balconies. Businesses and schools could provide gardens for employees and students to enjoy. Empty lots could be made into community gardens where young and old would share the responsibilities as well as the fun and fresh air.

Huge suburban and city-center parking lots could be transformed into small parks, community gardens, sports fields, and skating rinks. Neighborhood streets not needed as part of a transit corridor could be narrowed and the extra space used for gardens. Because traffic and pollution would be greatly reduced, vegetables and other edibles could be grown without the danger of accumulating harmful substances such as lead, asbestos, and rubber dust.

Did you know that a home garden can produce two to four times more food per acre than a big commercial farm? And the food is better-tasting, fresher, and more nutritious.

Plants and Trees. In ecocities, native plants are more important than imported plants that require a lot of care and watering. Ecocities would have very few grass lawns, which

Urban gardening is a good way to learn the benefits of green space. Children in Missoula, Montana (right), learn about city gardening through the MUD Project. And Newark, New Jersey, residents (left) have used urban gardening to rebuild decaying neighborhoods.

Healthy urban trees are an important part of an ecocity. They keep the air clean, absorb city noise, and provide food and homes for urban animals. When full grown, the tree these children are planting will help warm and cool the house.

eat up our time and water and encourage the use of chemicals. Instead, ecocities would have low-maintenance plantings along with fruit and nut trees, berry bushes, herbs, and vegetables.

Healthy trees are pretty—people feel better, more relaxed and friendly when trees are around. Also, trees may help stop global warming. First, they absorb carbon dioxide, the major greenhouse gas. Second, if planted in appropriate places, they can help us save energy and reduce fossil-fuel use. In summer, they are natural air conditioners—they provide us with shade and coolness. In winter, they are natural blankets—they keep our houses warmer.

Trees also provide food and homes for birds and small animals. They help fight noise pollution by soaking up sounds. A tree-lined street is a quieter place than a street with no trees, and the middle of a city park is quieter yet.

Conserving Energy and Resources

Ecocities will save energy and resources in many ways. The biggest way, of course, is that they rely more on "people power" for transportation than on cars. Public transportation also uses energy and materials much more efficiently than private cars. So just getting us out of our cars will save a tremendous amount.

In addition, ecocities will use a minimum of fossil fuels for other purposes. Instead, they will rely on renewable and less-polluting energy sources such as solar power, biomass (plant and animal waste used for fuel), hydrogen, and wind power. They will even have hydroelectric-power dams that will be small enough not to harm the environment.

Ecocity buildings are heated and kept cool more efficiently. They use more efficient motors to get work done, and they use energy-efficient lighting and appliances. They take advantage of the sun's natural ability to heat a space when heat is needed. They also take advantage of cooling breezes, open windows, window shades, and trees and shrubs to reduce heat from direct sunlight. Whenever possible, ecocity buildings will be made from local materials.

Reducing Waste. Curbside pickup of recyclable materials is easy and efficient in a compact city, so more paper, glass, metals, and plastics will be recycled. Composting (recycling foods, leaves, and other organic waste by turning it into a fertile, nourishing soil) will be a regular part of life. For example, we could all bring organic waste from our kitchens and our yards or gardens to community gardens where it would be composted to enrich the soil.

Ecocities will re-use and recycle entire buildings! Buildings that already exist and are in good shape will be protected and restored if possible. Re-using and recycling

Solar panels use the sun's nonpolluting energy for home heating and cooling (left). *Julia Russell, owner of Eco-Home in Los Angeles* (right), *works organic compost into her soil instead of using chemical fertilizers.*

building materials and structures saves energy, labor, and materials. It takes 14,000 BTUs (a BTU is a way of measuring energy) to make one single brick. The energy used to build a brick structure is wasted if the building is knocked down and the materials thrown away instead of being used again.

A Good Life

Ecocities will be designed as beautiful places to live and built with respect for all living things—plants, animals, creeks, and human beings of all sizes, shapes, colors, ages, and abilities. Everyone—young people, old people, and people who are sick or disabled or poor—will have better access to other people and places.

Ecocities will be quieter, safer, and cleaner than today's overcrowded city centers, but more interesting and easier to get around in than today's sprawling suburbs. Ecocities will offer more opportunities to be outdoors—with lots of parks and streams so we don't have to drive far to "get away."

People who live near each other will be able to know, watch out for, and help each other. There would be a feeling of friendliness and a sense of belonging to a neighborhood. This will help reduce many of today's urban problems such as crime, drug abuse, poverty, and homelessness.

Part of the reason cities aren't in better shape is that, all too often, people from outside the community—people with money and power—have made the decisions. That's how polluting incinerators get built near poor neighborhoods. That's how noisy, ugly, polluting highways cut neighborhoods in half. That's how homes get built too far away from jobs, and how housing becomes unaffordable. That's how our trolley systems were destroyed.

Ecocities will have public areas where town meetings can take place, where people can discuss and learn about ecology, the law, economics, politics, and how their cities are run. People will be able to feel part of a real community, giving democracy a better chance to work. They'll be better able to solve their problems together, to plan and build things together, to have more say in what goes on in their own neighborhoods . . . and affects their own world.

This idea of ecocities isn't just dreaming. The transformation of cities into ecocities is already starting to take place all over the world.

NASA scientists have designed "ecocities for space"—cities that will be totally self-sufficient and nonpolluting.

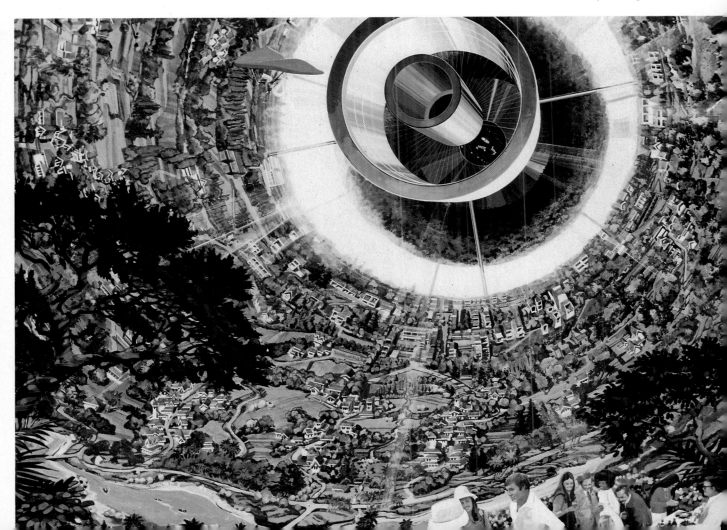

Chapter 8

Building Better Cities
Around the World

ECOCITIES SOUND PRETTY GOOD, don't they? Although no complete ecocities exist yet, hints that someday they will are showing up all over the world. A growing group of environmentalists, architects, city and regional planners, transportation experts, elected officials, scientists, ordinary concerned citizens, and young people are taking the first steps toward changing the way we build and live in our cities.

They are aiming to make our cities *sustainable*, which means that they don't take anything away from the Earth's environment, so that the next generation, and the next, will not find a deteriorated planet.

There are two basic ways of creating ecocities—building brand-new ones "from scratch" and reshaping cities that already exist. It's harder but more important to reshape existing cities. That way, we use a minimum of land and resources, and more people will be able to stay in the communities they live in now.

Because getting people out of their cars is a major goal of ecocity building, a lot of the redesigning is more for people and less for cars.

What's a Woonerf?

One way to change our transportation habits is to redesign existing areas to encourage walking and bicycling. *Woonerf* is a Dutch word for a street that has been turned into a place to be, rather than a route that gets you from one place to another. Hundreds of Dutch and German cities have used benches, trees, playgrounds, gardens, and sculptures to transform certain streets where cars are not permitted to go faster than pedestrians can walk.

This pedestrian-only street located in Bonn, Germany, leads to a large open market. Most European cities have similar areas where no vehicles are allowed.

Many other cities, especially in Europe, have developed pedestrian-only centers. Florence, Italy, for example, has turned its downtown into a pedestrian mall during the day.

Although Europe has a strong tradition of walking and biking, many cities face steadily worsening traffic jams and air pollution. The Netherlands now has over 9,000 miles (14,500 kilometers) of bike paths. In Japan, so many commuters bike to the train that stations have bike-parking towers—one is 12 stories high and holds over 1,500 bicycles!

FACT

Like many Third World cities where the residents can't afford cars, the capital city of Havana, Cuba, has twice as many bicycles as there are private cars on the entire island of Cuba. New bike lanes are marked on most main roads to handle the city's estimated 1 million bikes.

In the United States, about 40 percent of urban commuters drive less than 4 miles (6.5 kilometers) per trip. So biking could easily replace driving a car in many cases. One city that has made bike riding more attractive than driving a car is Palo Alto, California. The city pays its employees for each mile of biking they do while on business errands. It has closed 2 miles (3.2 kilometers) of a road to cars and turned it into a bicycle boulevard.

Improving Mass Transit

A growing number of cities are making public transportation such as light rail, subways, and buses, more available. For example, several have built, or are building, light-rail systems that link suburbs with downtown commercial areas.

Even Los Angeles, the leader in car-based communities, has realized that no matter how many more highways they build, or how they stagger work hours, they will still have traffic problems and bad air. Part of the answer, they decided, is for people to live closer to where they work and shop. And part of the answer is to put money and effort into other forms of transportation. That's why Los Angeles is investing $6 billion on a subway and light-rail system.

Paul Glover, an urban ecologist, wrote of Los Angeles that it is "an army camped far from its sources of supply, using distant resources faster than nature renews them. . . . Sooner or later it must generate its own food, fuel, water, wood, and ores. It must use these at the rate that nature provides them." He thinks that can happen.

High-speed rail systems between cities are being planned and built. So far, Europe and Japan lead the way. In the United States, Texas is taking the lead and hopes to have high-speed trains linking its largest cities by 1999. By 1995, Florida will build a line $13^{1}/_{2}$ miles (21.7 kilometers) long from the airport in Orlando to DisneyWorld. Florida's train will use magnetic levitation, or "maglev," to go 250 miles (400 kilometers) per hour.

FACT

In Manila, capital of the Philippines, a program started in 1975 to double the cost of gasoline. The government also built a light-rail line that covered most of the city. In the first eleven years, the consumption of gasoline dropped 43 percent. Manila, with 1,876,000 people, has most of the nation's cars.

Urban Gardening

A number of organizations are helping people create more green, open spaces in or near cities. Such spaces clean up the area, add beauty to often dreary lives, and give residents fresh vegetables they grow themselves.

In New York City, 750 community gardens have sprung up, thanks to help from the city agency Operation Green Thumb, as well as private groups. The groups supply seed money, information, equipment, and leases to unused city property. The gardens supply neighborhoods with much-needed open space—and about a half a million dollars in vegetables every year!

Similar urban garden organizations exist in many other cities, such as SLUG (San Francisco League of Urban Gardeners) and BUG (in Boston).

A growing number of groups all over the world plant trees in urban areas. Their goals are to improve the appearance of cities, to make them more comfortable to live in, and slow global warming.

These Guatemalan children are helping to turn their city green again by planting trees donated by the Trees for Life international organization.

TreePeople, a group in Los Angeles, is one of the most famous and successful. The group runs leadership programs for over 50,000 children, where they learn about planting and caring for trees, recycling, and composting. Many other cities have their own tree-planting programs.

The American Forestry Association has an Urban Forest Council that promotes urban tree planting. The association's goal is to plant 100 million trees in American cities by 1992. It's part of a large worldwide effort called Global ReLeaf, which gets volunteers of all ages to plant the trees in any open spaces available.

It's important to plant trees that are native to the area in which they are being planted. This will cut down on the need for extra water and help the trees survive in cities that have not yet turned into ecocities.

Planting Street Trees

An Earth Experience

Plant a tree near your home or school. There are so many places in a big city that need more trees. Not every kind of tree can survive being crowded with humans and their activities. A city tree should be able to withstand city dust, smoke, and pollution as well as poor soil; produce a good amount of shade; withstand seasonal changes whether it be hot/cold or wet/dry periods; provide fruits and seeds for city wildlife; produce flowers or fruits that don't have a foul smell; and resist diseases and insect damage.

Some common city trees that you might investigate include silver maple, linden or basswood, pin oak, Norway maple, poplar, London plane, ginkgo, and box elder.

Creeks, wetlands, and waterfronts are being restored in and around urban areas. In Berkeley, California, there was a forlorn abandoned lot with broken glass on the ground and a creek buried under it. A landscape architect, local residents, and environmental activists got together and decided to change the picture.

Now Berkeley has Strawberry Creek Park, which brings out the child in everybody. The creek is a lush, green, gurgling waterway, with a thriving crayfish population. Residents hope to be able to open up more parts of the creek and eventually get trout to return as well.

Transforming Downtowns

Twenty years ago, the downtown section of Portland, Oregon, resembled many city centers—it was sick and getting sicker. Stores were leaving the area. Streets were deserted after 5 P.M. Suburban developments were pulling more people away and creating the need for more highways. Traffic was choking the roads and poisoning the air.

But Portland didn't give up. It decided to put more money into a bus and rail system. Instead of a planned highway, it built a waterfront park. It tore down a big parking garage and built a piazza, an open square. It worked! Now, downtown car traffic has been reduced, the air is cleaner, and more people have come to work, shop, and relax in the downtown area.

Rock Hill, South Carolina, is transforming its downtown, an abandoned retail district, into a "pedestrian urban village." The plan was developed by citizens, agencies, and local institutions. The plan preserves historic buildings and adds new ones that fit the style of those that already exist.

A community art center, open-air farmer's market, and homes are included.

Urban Barn Raising

Barn raising is an old American tradition. Because a farmer working by himself could not carry long wooden beams for a barn, or raise up a wall from the ground and hammer it in place, he learned to rely on his neighbors. Building barns had to be a group effort.

Karl Linn, a landscape architect, has taken this idea and helped people use it to create community ecocity projects. For example, he helped students of the Massachusetts College of Art transform a parking lot into a green commons that could be used by the college and the community. With very little money (but a lot of sweat and cooperation), they used old bricks to build a patio and barbecue and planted a lawn and flower beds.

Linn also helped establish Neighborhood Commons organizations in Washington, D.C.; Baltimore, Maryland; Harlem, New York; Chicago, Illinois; and many other cities. They build public open spaces in low-income neighborhoods. Many of them include community vegetable and flower gardens, shaded sitting areas for older people, sandboxes for young children, dance areas for teens, and spaces for picnics, meetings, and celebrations. A neighborhood commons is a place where young and old can be in each other's presence, but not in each other's way.

In the 1920s, the river that flowed through San Antonio, Texas, was going to be paved over because it flooded the city. But a local architect convinced city officials to keep the river. It's now the center point of a beautiful, internationally famous shopping and walking area.

A program called *A Kid's Place* asked the question: "How can we make Seattle a better place for kids to live?" City officials asked kids to rate the city—where is the cleanest, the dirtiest, the most boring place? The city used the responses to plan new bus routes that would take kids where they wanted to go without having to be driven. In addition, the waterfront is being rebuilt to make it a nicer place to visit.

Redesigning Ecocity Homes

The Eco-Home, in Los Angeles, is a model home that shows what you can do with a small piece of land and an ordinary little California bungalow. Julia Russell, the owner, has redesigned the house and garden to be environmentally sound and more energy efficient than those of her neighbors.

The front yard is landscaped with plants that can survive on rain alone, rather than needing water from a garden hose. The garden and orchard have vegetables and fruit trees, watered by a drip-irrigation system that conserves water by dripping it to each plant instead of all over. Trimmed branches from the trees provide firewood. Leaves and kitchen scraps are composted and used to enrich the garden soil. The garden and orchard supply 50 percent of Russell's food in summer and 20 to 25 percent in winter.

Fruit trees shade the west side of the house, keeping it cool in summer. They shed their leaves in winter, allowing the sun to warm the house. Because she plants a diverse mix of useful plants, insects are kept away naturally.

The Eco-Home has photovoltaic (solar) cells that capture the sun's energy for overhead lights, and rooftop panels of

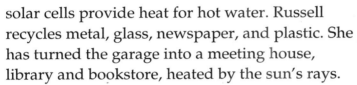

solar cells provide heat for hot water. Russell recycles metal, glass, newspaper, and plastic. She has turned the garage into a meeting house, library and bookstore, heated by the sun's rays.

Many homes in cities and suburbs could be transformed into just such eco-homes. Even a start, such as planting trees, is better than leaving things the old way.

A California organization called Urban Ecology is encouraging the development of what they call *integral neighborhoods*. They define them as neighborhoods that "foster local energy and food production, resource conservation, economic self-reliance, and community care and cooperation." Study the drawing on the next page and see how many listed characteristics of such a neighborhood you find.

Fruit from Eco-Home's orchards is dried (left) *by the sun for winter use. Fresh vegetables* (right) *grow in flower beds fertilized with compost.*

New Cities "from Scratch"

Some people are creating brand-new cities and ecological communities on new land. Although in general, this is more wasteful than transforming existing cities, this approach is still better than building suburbs. A lot of people like these new communities and want to live in them. Maybe if enough people think they're a good idea, more people will use the same ideas to change cities that have already been built.

What's in an Integral Neighborhood?

1. mixed-used buildings
2. rooftop garden
3. rooftop recreation areas
4. community garden
5. urban shade trees
6. fruit and nut trees
7. photovoltaic cells
8. wind turbine
9. neighborhood recycling center
10. compost bin
11. solar panels
12. chicken coop
13. light-rail mass transit
14. pedestrian/bicycle street
15. electric vehicle
16. walking/running paths
17. neighborhood playgrounds
18. neighborhood food cooperative
19. neighborhood bulletin boards
20. bleachers
21. neighborhood meeting
22. urban orchard
23. bridges connecting buildings
24. rainwater collection barrels
25. tanker ship using wind-powered sails
26. rooftop cafes
27. neighborhood design group

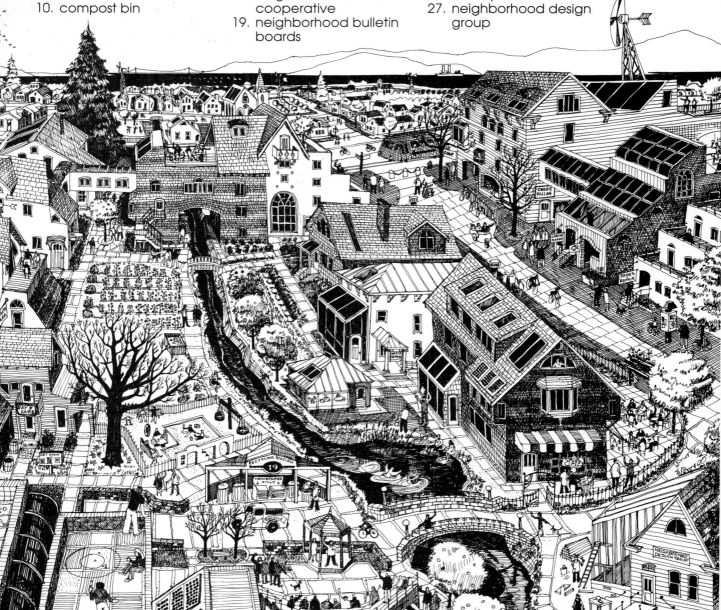

Arcosanti will be an entire city within a single structure. The city's parts will be connected and little land or natural resources will be used. Everything will be recycled so there will be no waste.

Arcosanti means "before things" in Italian—referring to a time before humans became crazy about owning things. It is the name given to an town planned by an architect, Paolo Soleri, now being built in the high desert between Phoenix and Flagstaff, Arizona. The goal is to create a city for 5,000 people that does the most with the least.

Since the design is so compact, it conserves heat and energy. Arcosanti will have a large solar greenhouse on the south slope providing heat for the buildings and using one-tenth the water that open-air farms would require.

Living areas are on the outside of the structure, facing the natural landscape. Transportation consists of bridges and elevators that connect different wings. The town will include homes, workplaces, cafes, schools, and entertainment.

Arcosanti will be very dense—200 people per acre (0.4 hectare). This is much higher than even New York City, which many people think is too dense. But since Arcosanti will waste no space on streets, parking lots, garages, or gas stations, people will have more living space than you think.

Cerro Gordo in Oregon is a "from-scratch" ecovillage that will combine village, farm, and forest. They have begun

The designers hope that Kentlands, Maryland, will be like an old-fashioned hometown. It will have neighborhood parks, corner stores, lakes for everyone to enjoy, schools, and a downtown city center. Clustered homes will be near offices, and both will be near shopping.

building clustered solar homes with a courtyard on one side and natural meadow and forest on the other.

The community will be self-supporting. Organic gardens will supply most of their food. They plan to create enough jobs for everyone, and they already have a company that makes bicycle trailers which are shipped all over the world. Cerro Gordo will minimize resource use and maximize re-use and recycling, relying on wind, water, and solar energy.

Yet another "from-scratch" idea is called the "New Traditional Small Town." Developers, urban designers, and public officials are experimenting with building new towns inspired by old European and nineteenth-century American small towns. Seaside, on the Gulf of Mexico in Florida (see page 88), is the first completed example.

The architects of these and other new town projects, Andres Duany and his wife Elizabeth Plater-Zyberk, believe that "most of the needs of daily life can be met within a 3- to 4-acre [1.2- to 1.6-hectare] area, and generally within a 5-minute walk of a person's home."

Another promising alternative to the suburb comes from Peter Calthorpe, a San Francisco architect and town planner, who has developed the "Pedestrian Pocket." This balanced, high-density, mixed-use "town" is based on homes built within walking distance of the central square, shopping and business, medical centers, parks, and a light-rail station.

A big project of Calthorpe's based on this idea is Sutter Bay, currently underway. It will consist of 14 villages, 10 miles (16 kilometers) north of Sacramento, California. Sacramento will extend its new light-rail transit system from the city center to Sutter Bay.

Design Your Own Ecocity

An Earth Experience

You can either make your own new city up completely "from scratch," or transform the area you live in using ecocity principles.

Remember, feet first! Design your ecocity so that people can walk to most places. Next, people should be able to ride bikes, skateboards, or roller-skate around. For longer distances, be sure to include streetcars, buses, special vans, and even ferryboats if your city is near water.

Don't forget to have lots of open space and green spaces where people can meet, relax, and enjoy being outdoors. Parks, creeks, roof gardens, nearby farms—all can be part of your ecocity.

Will you let people drive any cars at all in your ecocity? If you do, how fast will they go? Will they be able to go everywhere? Can people park everywhere—or will they park outside town and use another way to get around the city? What kind of energy will your city use: electric, solar, wind, water?

Draw the plans for your ecological city of the future.

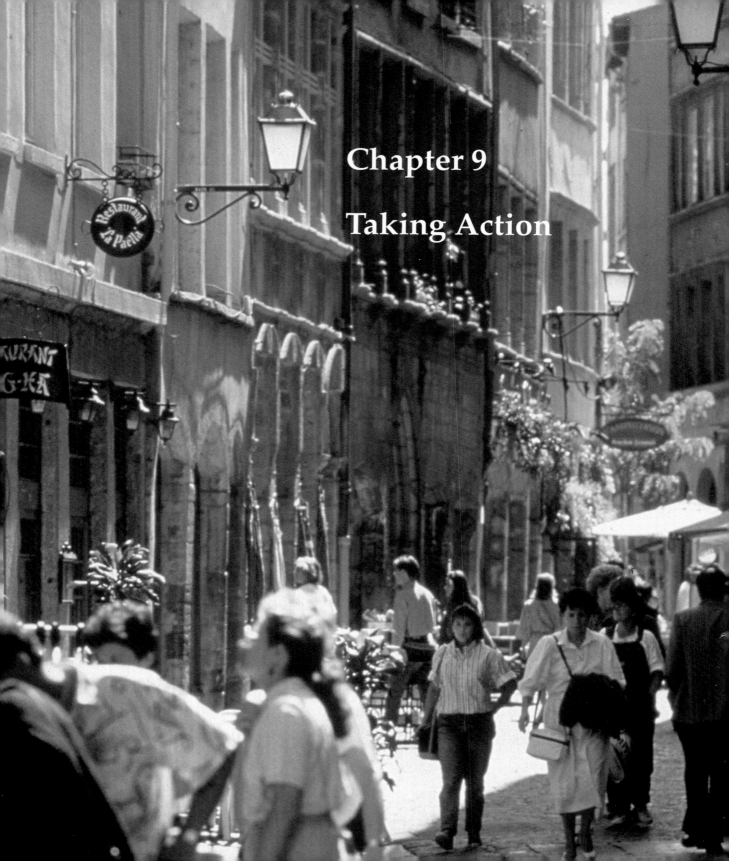

Chapter 9
Taking Action

EARTH'S HUMAN POPULATION GREW from 1 million persons 5,000 years ago to 5.3 billion today. Our success has been partly due to our ability to adapt and change, to live together in communities, to cooperate with each other to create great things, and to shape our environment.

Unfortunately, the urban environment we have created is turning out to be more harmful than most human beings and other forms of life on this planet. If we are to survive, we must change the way we have been thinking about and building our cities. You can play a role in those changes.

Taking Personal Action

Taking action to help the environment is important, but you can't do it alone. Talk to your family members about making these changes in your life.

Save Energy on Transportation

1. Try to live closer to where your parent(s) work.
2. Walk to as many places as possible.
3. Bike or take public transit whenever possible.
4. If your family uses a private car, try to carpool with other people, or arrange schedules so you combine errands and save on driving.
5. Whenever possible, work at home or telecommute by computer and fax machines.
6. Encourage employers and schools to support people who don't drive by reimbursing them for using a bike or public transit, or by providing shuttle vans.
7. Start a petition for car-free areas and bicycle routes in your town or city.

It saves time and money when workers commute to jobs together. Many urban highways have special express lanes for commuters who pool rides in cars, vans, and buses.

8. Rent cars or share them with other people, but only when there is no other way to get somewhere.

9. Discuss with your family the possibility of selling the car if you have one—or can you share one with another family?

10. If you can't give up a car, keep it tuned and running smoothly.

11. If you buy a new car, choose one that gets good mileage, at least 35 miles per gallon (15 kilometers per liter).

12. If you have a car with an air conditioner, give the air conditioner up rather than having it repaired and refilled with CFCs.

13. Consider buying an electric car for those times when a car is needed.

Spread the Word

1. Talk to your friends at school and your family members about cities and the environment.

2. Speak up at local hearings where new urban development is being discussed.

3. Take part in early planning stages of local projects.

4. Talk to your mayor, and contact local real-estate developers and ask what impact their next project will have on the environment.

5. Create your own local ecocity group. There's strength in numbers, working together to solve your environmental problems, coming up with better ideas than one person working alone might develop.

6. Contact the Healthy Communities Project at the

address on page 122 if you are interested in finding out how your city can become part of this international program.

Make Your City Greener

1. Switch to native drought-resistant species for your garden or lawn. Ask local nurseries and gardening supply stores for suggestions on good species for your region.

2. Grow some of your own food in a backyard, front yard, patio, or rooftop garden.

3. Look for an unused empty lot near your home. Maybe you can help turn it into a community garden or pleasant green open space for the community to pitch in and enjoy. You will need special permission to change the lot, so get help from an adult.

4. What about starting a garden at your school? Or suggest that your parents start one at work.

5. Plant your garden to attract local wildlife. Ask for information from a nursery, your local chapter of the National Audubon Society, or the National Wildlife Federation.

6. Plant trees in your city and around your home. For Christmas, buy a live tree in a pot that you can plant out-

Many people are becoming more self-reliant in cities by raising part of their food in gardens. It saves money, makes cities "greener," and helps relieve the stress of living in cities.

119

doors afterward, or find out how to recycle your tree in your community.

7. Be sure to take care of the trees you plant until they are big enough to survive on their own.

8. Avoid using chemicals on your plants.

Turn Your Home into an Eco-Home

1. Check with your gas and electric company for energy-saving tips such as insulation and energy-saving lighting. (But avoid foam insulation made with CFCs.)

2. Plan a group or family trip to one of the new environmental stores that are being started. Many of them have catalogs of environmentally responsible items.

3. Recycle as much as you can at home and suggest your family and school does, too.

4. Build a home recycling center.

5. Consider installing a greenhouse room or solar panels on your roof.

6. Make sure no one in your home *ever* pours chemicals or car oil onto the ground, down the drain, or into a sewer.

7. Compost kitchen scraps and yard waste and use the resulting material in your garden or potted house plants. Or donate it to community gardens.

Common products used in the home contain hazardous chemicals. Alternatives can be used safely and effectively without polluting the environment.

8. To avoid releasing CFCs into the atmosphere, make sure that the CFCs are recycled when your home or car air conditioner or your refrigerator is repaired.

Writing Letters

Throughout most of the world, ordinary people realize that something must be done to stop the continued degradation of our planet. Our politicians and lawmakers are only beginning to get the message.

In 1990, the United States strengthened the Clean Air Act of 1970, a step in the right direction. But the legislation still doesn't tell us *how* to reduce air pollution.

Let the people in power know about how important it is to change our cities if we are going to save our environment. Write:

1. To elected officials, urging that they support laws promoting energy efficiency, renewable energy (solar, wind);

2. To car manufacturers, urging them to develop alternatives to the combustion engine;

3. To government officials and developers, to expand the number of public and community gardens in cities;

4. To the editors of newspapers, and magazines; to radio or TV shows; to local real estate developers;

5. To local and state government to provide more public transportation.

Join Organizations

Many national environmental organizations work on improving our cities, especially transportation and air pollution. Here are some suggestions of groups you might join:

Auto Free Cities, 270 Lafayette #400, New York, NY 10012

Campaign for New Transportation Priorities, 236 Massachusetts Ave., NE, Suite 603, Washington, DC 22202

Eco-Home, 4344 Russell Ave., Los Angeles, CA 90072

Environmental Defense Fund, 257 Park Ave. South, New York, NY 10010

Global ReLeaf Program, American Forestry Association, P.O. Box 2000, Washington, DC 20013

Greenpeace, 1436 U St., NW, Washington, DC 20009, or 185 Spadina Ave., 6th floor, Toronto, Ontario, Canada M5D 2Z5

Healthy Communities Project, c/o National Civic League, 1445 Market St. #300, Denver, CO 80202-1728 or 126 York St. #104, Ottawa, Ontario, Canada K1N 5T5

National Audubon Society, 801 Pennsylvania Ave., SE, Suite 301, Washington, DC 20003

National Clean Air Coalition, 1400 16th St., NW, Washington, DC 20036

Natural Resources Defense Council, 40 W. 20th St., New York, NY 10011

National Wildlife Federation, 1412 16th St., NW, Washington, DC 20036

Planet Drum/Green City Program, P.O. Box 31251, San Francisco, CA 94131

Sierra Club, 730 Polk Street, San Francisco, CA 94109

TreePeople, 12601 Mulholland Drive, Beverly Hills, CA 90210

Urban Ecology, P. O. Box 10144, Berkeley, CA 94709

Youth Action, 2385 18th St., NW, Washington, DC—Youth Action acts as a clearing house for environmental youth groups.

Remember, building ecocities and living in them will play an important part in shaping the future of the entire planet.

GLOSSARY

acid rain – rain and other precipitation that is more acidic than normal because of air pollution.

city center – the part of a city where the buildings are closest together and most business and entertainment take place.

ecology – the study of how living things interact with each other and their environment.

ecosystem – a specific environment and the living things that inhabit it.

energy conservation – making the supply of energy last longer by using less.

erosion – the wearing away of soil or rock by wind and water.

extinction – the death of an entire species of plant or animal.

fossil fuel – a source of energy—coal, oil, natural gas—that was made over millions of years from dead and decaying living things, mostly plants.

global warming – the gradual rise in Earth's average temperature beyond normal limits, caused by the addition of excess greenhouse gases in the atmosphere, especially from burning fossil fuels and cutting forests.

greenhouse effect – the warming of the Earth's atmosphere because certain gas molecules trap heat from the sun. It keeps our planet habitable.

groundwater – underground water, which feeds wells and springs and which we can pollute.

habitat – the place where a species normally lives.

herbicide – a chemical that kills plants, especially unwanted plants such as weeds.

incineration – planned and controlled burning, usually of trash.

landfill – a place where solid waste is dumped and buried. It is usually lined to prevent polluted rainwater from running through it into the ground.

municipal waste – solid and liquid garbage from a town or city; usually does not include industrial waste.

ozone layer – that portion of the stratosphere where ozone molecules collect. It protects us from harmful ultraviolet rays of the sun.

pesticide – a chemical that is used to kill pests, especially insects and rodents.

pollute – to make dirty or unhealthy

public transit – public transportation for large groups of people: buses, trolleys, trains, ferries, and subways.

recycling – the process of reusing materials that would otherwise be thrown away, especially paper, plastic, steel, aluminum, and glass. It includes collection, remaking into new products, and the marketing of those products.

resource – something that supports life. A natural resource is one found on or in the Earth.

runoff – rainwater or irrigation water that collects whatever oil, pesticides, fertilizers, lead, or other chemicals are on pavement or land and carries them into lakes, rivers, and oceans.

smog – hazy, polluted air, originally found only in big cities but now even endangering crops. A combination of the words "smoke" and "fog."

stratosphere – the upper layer of the Earth's atmosphere, of which the ozone layer is a part; located above the troposphere where weather occurs.

suburbia – the total fringe area of a city, and the way of life of the suburbs.

suburbs – the villages and towns located along the outer edge of a city, where buildings are spread out.

topsoil – the fertile top layer of soil that contains the nutrients plants need to grow.

urban – city-like, or related to cities.

urban ecology – the study of living things in the city environment, and of the city in its larger environment—the state, the region, the country, the world.

INDEX

bold number = illustration

PHOTO SOURCES

Air India Library: 56, 91 (bottom)
American Petroleum Institute: 34
Archives of Ontario/AO686, AO687: 24, 25
Dr. Gary Benson: 17, 28, 45 (left), 71 (bottom right)
Brazil Tourism Office: 91 (top)
British Tourist Authority: 96
Dave Buchen: 39, 69
California Department of Water Resources: 41
State of California/Department of Transportation: 2, 10, 35
Colorado State Department of Health: 65
The Community Redevelopment Agency of the City of Los Angeles: 9 (left)
COSANTI: 113
Courtesy of the Danish Tourist Board: 74
Andres Duany/Elizabeth Plater-Zyberk, Architects: 88, 114
S.C. Delaney/EPA: 68
Mark Edwards/PANOS: 45
Owen Franken/German Information Center: 104
Food & Agriculture Organization/J. Isaac: 71 (bottom left)
French Government Tourist Office: 116
German Information Center: 14
Greenpeace: 46
Carrol Henderson: 42 (left)
Jeanine Hess: 50, 64 (both), 71 (top left)
The Indianapolis Project, Inc./Delores Wright: 75
Inter-American Development Bank: 21
Japan National Tourist Organization: 6
The Lindsay Museum: 76, 81 (right)
LiphaTech Inc.: 84
MUD Project/Brendon Moles: 97 (right)

National Aeronautics and Space Administration: 101
National Air Photo Library, Canada: 78 (both)
National Park Service: 80
New York Convention & Visitors Bureau: 9 (right), 87
New York State Department of Environmental Conservation: 48
City of Orlando, Florida: 102
Julia Russell/Eco-Home: 99 (both), 111 (both)
Rutgers Urban Gardening: 97 (left), 119
Salt Lake City Neighborhood Housing Services: 93
San Antonio Visitors & Convention Bureau: 109
San Francisco Convention & Visitors Bureau: 32, 73
Barrie Smith/French Government Tourist Office: 19
South Coast Air Quality Control Management District: 66 (both), 118
State Historical Society of Wisconsin: 16
Texas State Department of Health: 49
Trees for Life: 98, 106
Toronto Transit Commission: 23
U.S. Department of Housing & Urban Development: 13, 27, 42 (right)
U.S. Fish & Wildlife Service/Sue Matthews: 81
Dr. Louis Uehling: 11, 52, 58, 62, 63
United Nations Photo Library: 44, 71 (top right)
Wisconsin Department of Natural Resources: 120
World Bank Photo Library: 8, 12

ILLUSTRATIONS

Bill Mastin, Architect: 112

ABOUT THE AUTHOR

Nancy Bruning has been writing books and articles, mostly about how to get and stay healthy, for fifteen years. She was born and raised in Brooklyn, New York, and now lives in San Francisco with her husband, Michael Ross, and her cat, Simone. Nancy loves visiting the countryside, but prefers living in the city. She is working to make cities more ecologically healthy through her writing and through projects sponsored by Urban Ecology.